the *evangelist*

by Bob Hill

CR

Cross Reference Books
1100 NW Rutland Road
Mt. Juliet, TN 37122

Library of Congress Cataloging Number 80-067980

Copyright ~ 1980
Clyde Dupin Ministries
Second Printing, 1985
Third Printing, 1992
Fourth Printing, 1998

Published by **CROSS REFERENCE BOOKS**
1100 NW Rutland Rd. Mt. Juliet, TN 37122
Cover Design by Keith Fletcher
Graphics by Jan Fischer and Bill Smith

Contents

Chapter

Dedication

This book is graciously dedicated to the scores of God-called evangelists who have accepted the challenge to take the Gospel to "the ends of the earth." Especially, I dedicate this book to Clyde and Grace Dupin, whose lives have taught me the full meaning of what it costs to "do the work of an evangelist."

Introduction

When I first met Clyde Dupin, I immediately thought, "This man is unique. I want to know more about him." My wife, Georgia, and I sat with Clyde and his wife, Grace, while we sipped coffee in a hotel restaurant in Washington D.C. during the National Association of Religious Broadcasters annual meeting.

I continually fired questions to the Dupins because I was so intrigued with the exciting experiences of their lives. It was not his tall, gangly appearance, nor his Southern accent that attracted my attention, but rather his complete trust and faith in the God he proclaimed to millions of people through his evangelistic efforts. Here was a dedicated couple who really believed and lived the same gospel they preached across America and in several foreign countries.

"Clyde," I said, "you really ought to write a book about God's dealings in your life." He thought for a moment and then looked humbly into my eyes with a slight grin forming around his mouth.

"Bob," he replied, "I wonder who would be interested in reading a story about me. Furthermore, I just don't have the time to write a book. God has called me to be an evangelist, not an author."

I volunteered to write the book if he and Grace would sit down and tape record the intricate details of their lives. These tapes, interviews with friends and personal papers are the source of this heart warming story. This is the story of a farm boy, born in the hills of Kentucky near a little town (Eastview), you probably never knew existed. It is a story of God taking an insignificant, insecure boy and raising him up through trial and error to preach before many thousands of people who have come to know Jesus Christ personally.

From brush arbors to small country churches to a soccer stadium in Haiti with more than 45,000 packed into its seats and playing field, this story will thrill you as you see God at work today. You will share the thrills and the tears with the unique Dupin family and finish this book with a greater sense of God's presence in the world today.

I came away from that initial meeting having learned some valuable principles of Christian commitment. You also will learn greater trust, humility, dedication and discipleship as you read the story of a man who was called to be an evangelist.

Since that first meeting, my wife Georgia and I have been around the world with the Dupin team. We have witnessed thousands of people coming to Christ across America and in many parts of Russia, Croatia, Bosnia, as well as evangelistic crusades on several islands in the Caribbean.

And, God continues to use this extraordinary servant to reach the masses with the Gospel message. Let his story inspire you to witness aggressively for our Lord, Jesus Christ.

Bob Hill,
Mt. Juliet, Tennessee

Life on the Farm

1

Life on the Farm

The old pendulum clock that sat on the mantel downstairs struck six o' clock. It would be an hour before the sun would rise to burn the frost off of the barn roof and the other farm buildings. But that did not matter to Mr. Dupin. He believed in the old saying, "Early to bed, early to rise makes a man healthy wealthy, and wise." Kendrick Dupin wasn't wealthy but he certainly was wise. He believed the discipline of lots of hard work would form his sons into healthy and wise men.

He came to the bottom of the stairway and opened the wooden door that was stained around the knob from years of handling by unwashed hands. "Get up, boys," he called. "Time to milk the cows and feed the horses."

The crisp air of the Kentucky morning chilled the last remnants of sleep from young Clyde's eyes. Even so, he could have made his way to the barn without actually watching his steps, for he knew the path by heart.

Clyde was born on this farm in Hardin County, Kentucky, in the big front room of the old weather-beaten house on February 22, 1933, weighing eleven pounds, twelve ounces. His four older brothers, Hazel, Hubert, Cecil, Clayton, and a sister, Eula, were born in the same room. A younger sister, Clara, would be born there, too.

His dad's first wife had died leaving him with two sons and a daughter. Clyde was born to his second wife, Polly McGuffin, who in her unselfish, loving way had bonded the two families together as one. Polly was a large, lovely featured woman who knew only hard work and kindness to others. Kendrick Dupin, his father, was a farmer and was trusted and respected by all his neighbors.

"I'm not sure when our house was built," Clyde says. "The big front room, as we called it, was built before the turn of the century." For many years it had stood proudly on the hill as a two story log cabin. Later other rooms were added until it could boast six rooms and the complete house was then covered with weather boarding. There was no electricity or running water in their home.

There was a well in the back yard that provided water for the family by lowering a bucket on a chain and then pulling it back up again after the pail had been filled. Sometimes in long, hot, dry summer months the water would vanish from the well and Clyde would have to carry water from the spring down the hill below the house.

After his sixth birthday, he walked fearfully down the road to the little one-room schoolhouse. His fears were well founded, because his older brother, Hubert, was the teacher.

Hubert believed that learning took place best in an orderly, well disciplined classroom; so the "hickory stick," which he never hesitated to use, even on his youngest brother, was part of the curriculum.

Miss Edith came to the one-room schoolhouse when Clyde was in the fourth grade. Miss Edith not only taught the "three R's" but she also taught from the same Bible that she carried to the little white Baptist church on Sunday.

Clyde would study at night by the kerosene lamp that barely gave off enough light to shove the darkness from the far corners of the room; but he had such a great desire to learn that after his homework was completed, he sat for hours looking up new words in the "Webster's Dictionary," learning the meanings of them. Those early years were hard and were never forgotten, but they formed the character of the man for the whole of his life. It was then, at the earliest beginnings, that Clyde learned never to give up when life was hard. He learned that you will not always win; but if you keep trying, you will also know the joys and rewards of success.

In spite of the hard times there were many good times in his memory. Clyde remembers the cold winter evenings when the family sat around the big coal burning stove eating buttered popcorn which his mother had piled high in a large dishpan, listening to his dad strumming his guitar and singing old ballads that had been passed down by one generation to the next.

Clyde's Conversion

"I was a nine year old boy when exciting news was brought to us by a neighbor," Clyde remembers. It was September, 1942. There was going to be a tent meeting down the road from his house, about a mile. Truly, this was exciting news for a rural community that had "preaching" in most country churches only every fourth Sunday.

The first service of the tent meeting started on Sunday evening. Clyde, with his mother, brother, and sister went early so there would be plenty of time to visit with their neighbors before the revival services started.

There was an air of excitement as they gathered under the tent that night. The song leader took his place behind the pulpit. He told the congregation to "pull out all the stops," to sing loud. They did!

"Revive us again" was sung with great enthusiasm. They progressed from one hymn to another until it was time for the evangelist to preach.

When the young minister, Rupert Goodman, rose to speak, Clyde was impressed with the earnestness and fervor with which he preached. His message was simple and direct. "Who's side are you on? Are you with Jesus or against Him? Do you let Jesus rule your life or Satan? The Bible says, 'He who is not for me is against me.' Do you really let Him rule your life?" Rupert asked.

Clyde thought about these things as he walked home that night. "From my earliest memory I had always prayed," he remembers. "No one taught me to pray, because my mother and dad were not Christians. I just found that deep within me was a hunger for God, so I prayed. Also, deep within my soul was the awareness that God wanted me for a special work."

When he was a young child, even the neighbors must have sensed God was preparing Clyde for a special work, because they would point to him and say, "There goes Happy Chandler," (the governor of Kentucky at that time). Others would call him Billy Sunday.

"I knew I would be neither. I knew God was calling me into the ministry. I, alone, must answer that calling," Clyde says.

How worried he was as he went to the barn Thursday evening to do his chores. It had rained all day and the young lad was sure his folks would not let him go to the tent meeting that night. Oh, how he wanted to go back. He had not missed a service, but was afraid tonight he would have to stay home.

"I guess God knew this was to be a special night for me; for when I had finished my chores and stepped out of the barn, the rain had stopped and the sun popped out from behind the clouds," Clyde remembers.

He arrived early, as usual, for the revival service. He noticed a tall, handsome soldier in full dress uniform standing just outside the tent. World War II was on at that time and the army base, Fort Knox, was only about forty miles from his community

A Soldier Friend.

Before he could find a seat Clyde felt a big hand gently laid on his shoulder. It was Bruce Meads, the soldier from Fort Knox.

"Son do you know Jesus Christ as your Savior? Are you a Christian?" he asked. For a moment it startled Clyde. Then he answered him honestly, "No, sir, I am not a Christian?" That night he listened with rapt attention to Rupert's strong, urgent voice as he preached about coming judgment. "Are you ready?" he asked pointing his finger toward the audience.

Though Clyde was fully clothed in blue denim jeans and a blue cotton shirt, it seemed he stood naked before God that memorable night. Only his soul was naked. "You need not fear this judgment," Clyde heard the preacher saying, "If you fear, repent, and let Christ come into your heart. Decide now and then come forward and let us pray together."

Without hesitation the nine year old stepped out and went forward. Bruce Meads went with him and knelt by his side. As he repented of his sins and invited Christ into his life, he was born again.

Little did Clyde realize that night what a source of strength and encouragement this young soldier would become to him. Bruce Meads had no way of knowing that night he would soon be shipped overseas to Ireland. In the Battle of Kasserene Bass he would be captured by the German Army and sent to prison. From this prison he would be allowed to write only two letters a month. One he would write to his mother in Michigan and the other to Clyde, just to encourage him, a nine year old boy, in his new found faith.

The stars never looked so bright as Clyde walked out from under the tent that night. He had never felt so "good." He felt a new peace, and was so happy to be part of the family of God, that he wept for joy. Clyde hurried home to tell his parents about his commitment to Christ. He was sure they, too, would be saved that very night. But to his great disappointment this would have to come later. It would be a year later before his mother made this commitment, and it would be many years, after much fasting and praying, before his dad would come to know Christ.

The local Methodist Church had a summer revival and so did the Baptists. But they were always careful to schedule these at different dates, so the Methodists could visit the Baptist revival and the Baptists could visit the Methodist's. After he became a Christian, Clyde looked forward to the summer revivals with great anticipation. He didn't want to miss a night of these services.

Some nights part of the family would go with him to these meetings. Other nights he would walk the three miles alone. He would leave home happy and brave with a song in his ten year old heart; but he can still remember the fear that crawled up his spine on the way home.

As he passed the graveyard, his lantern cast ghostly shadows across the dark road in front of him. He would always say to himself, "I'll not go back tomorrow night." But he always did.

God sent many people to influence and encourage the young Christian in his new faith. Jimmy Goodman is one whom he'll never forget. Brother Jimmy, as he was affectionately called, was an old white haired Nazarene minister, who had moved into the community soon after Clyde was saved. Many afternoons Clyde would go to his house. They would study God's Word together. Clyde was a young boy and he an old man, separated by a great span of years; but a bond of love and respect grew between them.

Brother Jimmy became one of Clyde's dearest friends. It was through his influence and prayers that Clyde discovered the secret of the Spirit filled life. He urged him to serve God no matter the cost. Clyde told him he would! He told Brother Jimmy he was called to preach. "There is no higher calling. Never stoop to do anything else," he encouraged.

The Boy Preacher

2

The Boy Preacher

After Clyde had shared with Brother Jimmy that he had been called by God to preach, he felt a burning desire to share this wonderful joy that was in his heart with others. It seemed it would be a long time before he would be old enough to go away to college to learn how to preach, so why should he wait? Why not just start now and preach all the way to college, and right through college. So that is what he did.

Everyone in his community soon knew that Clyde Dupin was called to preach. He told his mother and dad. He told his neighbors, his friends, his teachers and he told every one who would listen that he was called to preach. Exciting things began to happen the next summer after he was saved. Brother Jimmy Goodman felt God wanted him to build a permanent place to have community-wide revivals. This was built across the road from where the tent had stood the summer before.

The farmers of the community, under the supervision of Brother Jimmy, took large posts and dropped them into holes they had dug. These posts would support the roof. When the structure was finished it took on the appearance of an open-air tabernacle. Benches for the people to sit on were made from rough boards. It was under this rough-hewn, open-air tabernacle that Clyde spent many happy hours each summer. He was the self-appointed janitor, and he would go early and dust the benches. He would stay late and go down each row, gather all the songbooks and stack them neatly near the front. He would pick up all paper or trash that had been dropped by careless persons.

To young Clyde this old tabernacle was a very hallowed place. It was a joy to keep it neat. In mid-summer of each year an evangelist would be invited to come and preach each evening for two weeks. There were day services, also. These day services were an opportunity for the local pastors to preach. It was in one of these afternoon services that the young preacher would attempt to preach his very first sermon.

Word spread fast in the community that the Dupin boy was going to preach at the tabernacle Monday. It was a beautiful warm, sunny afternoon when Clyde arrived at the tabernacle in his new white pants and white shirt that his mother had purchased for this very special occasion. People were already seated under the shade of the tabernacle, others still standing outside visiting with their neighbors. It looked like a great crowd to the new preacher, but was not nearly as large as his young eyes had envisioned it to be.

Short Sermon

All too soon the singing was over, the prayers prayed, the offering taken and he heard Rupert Goodman saying, "Ladies and gentlemen, it is with great joy that I present to you a boy preacher. This is his very first sermon." Then he turned and looked at Clyde sitting in a large chair behind him. He was so small his feet barely touched the rough board platform beneath him.

"Alright, Clyde, you preach for us," he said. Clyde had never been so nervous and afraid in his whole young life. Suddenly, he wondered if God had made a mistake calling him, a humble farm boy, to preach. But it was too late. He could not back out now because his neighbors and relatives were all staring at him with anxious expectation. He cleared his throat and tried to swallow the lump that had formed there.

"Friends and neighbors," he said in a high pitched voice, "turn to First John, chapter one." This was the only chapter in the Bible in which he was sure he could pronounce all the words. He read the entire chapter. This was the longest part of Clyde's sermon. He made a few remarks explaining God love for us, that we must repent of our sins and trust Him. Clyde thought he had prepared a sermon to last a half hour, but he ran out of anything to say in five minutes. The young preacher was very embarrassed because of the shortness of his sermon. This was a beginning, though a feeble one.

Revival Preacher

But as the young preacher approached his teens, age and experience helped him to improve greatly. Many ministers began to invite him to preach in their churches. He was invited to preach for the Methodist Church and the Baptist Church down the road from his house. Also, the Nazarene Church and Wesleyans invited him to speak in their churches. God was preparing Clyde then to do the work of interdenominational crusades that would come later in his life, even though he did not realize it at that time.

Many people came forward to accept Christ in those churches where he preached. This encouraged other ministers to invite the young preacher to speak. Soon, he had more invitations than he could accept. However, everyone was not pleased with his preaching. He remembers one minister in his community had asked him to preach for his church group. After he had finished preaching he called Clyde to the side and said, "Clyde, you have a great ability and you can someday pastor large churches if you will quit this preaching on being born again. Stop preaching about a personal salvation and repenting of your sins."

"I thought about what the man said" Clyde says. "It was discouraging to me, just a boy in my teens, to have an older minister talk to me in this manner, but I decided that day if I never had a large church to pastor, if I never had great audiences to preach to, even if I had to preach on a street corner, I would not compromise. I would preach the Bible like it was. I determined at that early age the Bible would always be my textbook."

All Aboard

3

All Aboard

The young preacher's mother and his sister, Clara, saw him to the Elizabethtown train station on a warm August morning in 1947. His mother had gotten up early to fix them a hot breakfast. It was one of those moments that would be as vivid and real in his mind years later as it was that warm summer day. That particular look of love and longing in his mother's eyes, the hissing of the wood burning in the big iron cook stove, the melted butter and the fresh blackberry jelly on hot steaming biscuits. Clyde would miss them.

His dad called from the front room, "Time to go, son. Harve is waiting outside." Harve was a neighbor who had agreed to take the three of them, with all Clyde's baggage to the train station, which was eighteen miles from their home. Finally, all his boxes and bags were pushed and shoved into the small trunk of Harve's old green Chevy car. Clyde turned to see the weather-beaten face of his dad.

"I saw tears of love, pride and, perhaps, concern in his eyes," Clyde remembers. "I was only fourteen and leaving the security of our home tucked away in the rolling hills of

Kentucky to attend a Christian academy in Northern Indiana. This was enough to bring concern to any father's heart. But Dad had finally consented to let me go after I persuaded him that God was calling me to preach and nothing could or would stop me."

Harve gave an impatient, loud roaring to the motor of the old Chevy, indicating it was time to get the good-bye over and be on their way. In the bright orange glow of the warm morning sun, the little gray, weather-beaten railroad station seemed to take on a new importance that Clyde had never noticed before. Walking along the wide platform that surrounded the station that August morning, the elation he felt was so great that he never thought to be embarrassed about the shabby and strange array of luggage and boxes that Harve was piling high on a railway wagon.

Clyde's mother had put handmade quilts, blankets, pillows, sheets and many other articles that he would need for his room at boarding school in a large cardboard box that she had gotten from the grocery store. The sides were bulging so badly and fearing they would burst, they stopped on the way to the train station and bought a rope to tie the box together.

Big Dreams

Soon Clyde was mounting the steps to the coach section of the train. The large, powerful L & N engine would be pulling the train that would carry the young preacher away into a whole new world. He found an empty seat by the window next to the train station. He saw his mother standing on the platform talking to the old conductor. Once, she pointed in his direction so he knew from long experience what she was saying, "That's my preacher boy in there. One of the best in the country. He's going away to school. Now, you take care of him." she told the nodding conductor.

Clyde was often embarrassed by his mother's glowing reports to complete strangers about her "preacher boy." But, as he looked at her through the train window that morning his mother's large frame body was neatly attired in a new dress she had ordered from Spiegel's Catalog. Her snowy white braids were softly framing her lovely face. Tenderness for her welled up in him. Clyde forgave her for bragging to the conductor about her "preacher boy" who was on board his train. The whistle blew shrilly and then the conductor cupped his hand to his mouth and shouted, "All aboard!"

It seemed before he mounted the steps the train started moving forward. The car jerked forward, the one behind slamming into it. Finally the jerking and the bumping began to smooth out and he glanced out just in time to see his mother still waving with one hand and dabbing a handkerchief to her eyes with the other.

As the telephone poles were sliding past outside, scenes were floating before his young mind, scenes of happy times, building play roads in the dirt under the big apple tree in the orchard down the hill below his house; the times he had gotten his young sister, Clara, and her playmates together in his dad's toolshed and preached to them. The toolshed became his cathedral and he preached to the small upturned faces as though they were some great audience.

But as the train raced on and village after village slipped by, Clyde knew he would never be back to be a part of this life again. God and Clyde had big dreams, and with big dreams you must go on. You never give up. You never go back. "When I was a child, I spoke as a child, I understood as a child, I thought as a child; but when I became a man, I put away childish things." (1 Corinthians 13:11.)

How long he dreamed and mused of the past he didn't know. When he looked up he could see the train was approaching a large city. Louisville, Kentucky, was just in the distance with its great towering buildings, pushing into the sky. Here, Clyde would change trains and board the Pennsylvania Railroad Line which would take him on to his destination in Northern Indiana. Soon, the train was moving out of the great Louisville Train Station and crossing the broad, winding Ohio River into Indiana. There, it seemed the hills soon vanished and land spread out into great flat fields.

Country Boy's New World

Clyde could see acre after acre of tall green corn swaying in the summer breeze. His eyes could hardly drink in the miles of beauty fast enough. The sun was a huge, blazing ball of red as it was sinking over the edge of the rich land of Northern Indiana.

Summer twilight was coming as the train began to slow down. The engineer blew a long warning whistle as the conductor announced that they were coming into Frankfort. It was a small midwestern county seat town. The courthouse was in the center with stores lining all four sides of the downtown square, two story houses with porch swings, lots of kids and free running dogs. The train's wheels soon ground to a stop. Already his eyes were searching the dusk, searching the train station for the school officials that would be there to meet him.

As Clyde stepped off the train steps, he had hoped someone would be coming toward him with a friendly smile and an outstretched hand to welcome Clyde Dupin to Frankfort. But there was no one, absolutely no one, to greet him or to greet anyone else. He was the only passenger who had gotten off the train at the Frankfort station.

He glanced up and down the potholed street just beyond the train station. Maybe they were late in coming. All he saw was the flickering neon lights across the tracks that advertised,

"Beer, Food & Wine," hanging in the greasy window of an old run down tavern. Tattered, drunken men were slouched on a bench on the porch of the tavern. Farther down the tracks, he could see a factory. It was a large foreboding brick building, blackened with grime and dirt. Steam was hissing from its sooty pipes.

Clyde's baggage was tossed on a wagon standing alongside the train. He watched as the train began to move slowly down the rails, then with gathering speed, it was gone. The young preacher felt fear rising within him. He looked up and down the station platform, casting an uneasy glance toward the tavern across the street. He was afraid. He was hungry and lonely, but he was not alone. God was there with His reassuring promise, "Have not I commanded thee? Be strong and of good courage; be not afraid, neither be dismayed; for the Lord thy God is with thee whithersoever thou goest." (Joshua 1:9)

Grace

4

Grace

As the sun sank farther over the horizon and darkness was beginning to settle down, Clyde realized that no one from the school was coming for him. He walked into the train station and asked the ticket agent who sat behind the grilled window, "Could you tell me, has there been anyone here asking for a Clyde Dupin?"

"Nope," the ticket agent said without looking up from the paper he was reading.

"May I use your phone to call a taxi?"

"S'pose you can if you drop a dime in it," the agent answered, still continuing to read his paper.

Finally Clyde, with his luggage arrived safely at the school. He found his room. Ralph Oden, a friend he had met in Elizabethtown, Kentucky, whose father had pastored a church there, became Clyde's roommate. First thing the next morning Clyde was out exploring the campus. The buildings were old and a little run down. But the campus was blessed with huge oak trees that gave it a cool, restful appearance. What did it matter if the buildings were old? So was the house where he had always lived.

Clyde loved the school immediately. Its atmosphere was one of excitement and joy, its discipline was strict and its president, Rev. R.K. Storey, was a deeply spiritual man who had a keen insight into the hearts and minds of the young students. Rev. Storey had been a missionary in the Philippine Islands. During World War II he and his wife had been captured by the Japanese soldiers while standing by the grave of their little daughter who had died only hours before. They were imprisoned in Manila for three long, torturous years. It was soon after the war that he came to the Frankfort Bible College and Academy to be president.

A New Home

All of the teachers, like Rev. Storey, were dedicated Christians who felt a Christian education was one of the most valuable assets a young person could possess. This gave their courses an important practicality. The Academy and Bible College were on the same campus; so many activities were shared by both groups. One of these activities was chapel each morning. Everyone was required to go. But for Clyde it was the time of day he loved best. It was a time of joy and spiritual learning.

Often there were lectures and sermons by visiting pastors and evangelists, active men who knew all the problems in the field and gave the students the benefit of their vital experience. Many times there were powerful sermons preached in these chapel services that would put the fear of God on the whole student body.

Even the tired old buildings on campus seemed to know they were part of a training ground where young men and women were preparing for a battle that could not be side stepped--the battle of life. If you listened closely you might think you could hear the huge oak trees that shaded the campus humming, "Onward Christian Soldiers," as they swayed in the cool breeze.

Campus Jobs

Clyde's father had given him enough money to pay for half of his school bill. The rest he must earn on his own. This policy was followed for four years at the Academy. Soon after his arrival on campus he knocked on the Dean of Men's door, little dreaming the man behind that door would one day be one of his best friends.

"Come in," a voice invited. Clyde opened the door cautiously and stepped in. The man at the desk turned around slowly and leaned back in his chair. He must have been about thirty years old, six feet tall, heavy set, and had soft blue eyes that twinkled from a smiling face that glowed with a ruddy complexion.

"Hello, son," indicating with a nod of his head for Clyde to sit down. "I'm Boone Murphy, the Dean of Men. Can I help you?"

"Yes, sir. My name is Clyde Dupin and I need a job to pay for my school bill. Do you have any work available for students?"

Clyde didn't know there were many more jobs available than there were students who were willing to work.

"What kind of a job would you like, Clyde?"

Clyde realized that his previous farm experience of plowing fields, milking cows and cutting weeds would be of little value here on this campus, so he said, "I will take any kind of a job you have open."

"Good," said the dean mischievously. "I happen to have some openings. How would you like to sweep all the sidewalks before breakfast each morning? Or clean all the restrooms in the men's dorm and class building? Or, how would you like to sweep and dust the chapel each evening and mop and wax it on Saturday?"

"I will take all three," Clyde said to the surprised dean. So these three jobs, which paid 40 cents an hour, were his. Clyde and his roommate, Ralph, worked diligently before classes, starting in the morning and as soon as they were dismissed in the afternoon. Since there was no great demand by other students for these jobs they kept them for the next two years.

Clyde enjoyed making himself independent. He was not one to waste time. He was free of the pride that kept others from doing these menial jobs. Clyde was soon known on campus for his drive, his initiative, his strength and determination in the face of almost insurmountable obstacles. He believed God could move mountains and that God used people to move them. Clyde believed he was one of those people God was going to use. He asked for divine help, guidance, and direction daily.

Jail Ministry

The young student had a deep desire to do more than go to classes, to work hard, and to study. He wanted to be helping people to find Christ. The opportunity came sooner than he expected. He met an old Christian gentleman, Peter Otton, at the church where the students attended on Sunday. He said, "Clyde, I've heard you are a good preacher. How would you like to come with me this afternoon? I'm going over to visit the prisoners in the city jail."

Clyde had never seen inside a jail before, but he thought it would be a great opportunity to preach, so he accepted. The hardened prisoners groaned their displeasure when the jailer announced that a young boy preacher was going to speak to them. But they groaned even louder when old Peter Otton announced he and Clyde Dupin were going to sing, "What A Friend We Have In Jesus," before the sermon. The prisoners had a reason to groan because the entire "What A Friend We Have In Jesus" was sung in a terrible off-key monotone.

But Clyde was undaunted. He stood in the middle of the old gray corridor of cells and in a strong voice told the men quite simply that Jesus loved them, that He would forgive them of their sins and they could be free from the bondage of sin.

He said, "'All have sinned and come short of the glory of God'. Your sins are not too great for God to forgive."

Tears came to the eyes of some of the prisoners. They were convicted by the message of this very young preacher. Clyde continued to return to the jail with old Peter Otton week after week, month after month, until some of the prisoners became Christians.

The Local Taverns

Many Saturday evenings Clyde would get a friend to go with him to the local taverns. They went not for the purpose of drinking, but to pass out gospel tracts to the bleary-eyed patrons who sat slouched in the booths drinking their bottles of booze. You had to be twenty-one to enter the tavern. Clyde and his buddy were only in their teens, so they would slip in the front door as inconspicuously as possible and go to the very last booth or table in the tavern and start passing out their tracts to each startled person, telling them, "Jesus loves you and will save you from your sin."

Before Clyde could work his way back up to the front door of the tavern the bartender had spotted him. He came over to Clyde, took one of the tracts out of his hand, looked at it and then in a loud, angry voice yelled, "Boy, get out of here and don't come back!"

But Clyde did go back many times, slipping in the front door to pass out tracts. On one of these visits to the tavern, an old man sitting at the table with a glass of beer looked up at Clyde with tear-filled eyes and said, "Boy, can you help me?"

"No, but Jesus can."

"Please," the old man said, "Would you pray for me?"

Clyde knew that there was no way he could pray for the man in the tavern without the bartender seeing him. So he said in a low voice, "Sir, come with me. Let's go outside and pray." So together they went out behind the tavern, knelt down in the alley and prayed out to God for forgiveness for the wayward sinner. God answered their prayers.

But, too soon this exciting school year was over, and he would go home for the summer. These summer months were not wasted or whiled away at the swimming hole that was located on the neighbor's farm. Most of the boys in the community would go swimming on Sunday afternoon in this wonderful cool water that was a deep hole in the flowing creek, but Clyde would take all the speaking engagements he could get on Sunday.

Clyde learned to preach when his knowledge was still limited. He had one passion and that was to win souls--not to be great-- but just to win souls. During these summer months he helped his father plow the fields. Many times, he would stop his horses and kneel down in the fresh turned soil that would bring forth harvest and pray, "Oh, God, someday let me harvest many souls for you."

The summer Clyde was sixteen he had ridden 175 miles from his home to the district campmeeting of the Wesleyan Church at Maysville, Kentucky. He had never seen so much excitement and happiness in one place. It seemed this place must be somewhat like heaven would be. There was preaching services three times a day by some of the best preachers he had ever heard. During this campmeeting, the last Saturday afternoon was always reserved for a big youth rally. After he arrived at the camp the youth director asked him if he would speak for that rally.

When Saturday arrived Clyde was happy and excited for the opportunity to preach in such a sacred place. The pews were packed and an air of excitement filled the tabernacle. He had prayed, studied, and prepared. He asked God to help him as he rose to preach, and God did. Before he had finished preaching, people were weeping. The presence of God was very evident over the whole audience.

After the service had been dismissed that afternoon, Mrs. Houston, the district superintendent's wife, came rushing up to him saying, "Oh, Clyde, I must share this with you. About fifteen years ago my husband pastored a church in Elizabethtown, Kentucky. While we were visiting in some homes about 18 miles from Elizabethtown, we happened to stop at your mother and father's home when you were just a baby. I took you on my lap to hold you. When I did, I felt God impressed upon me someday you would be mightily used of God. I prayed God's blessing on you that day."

He had never heard this story before, but it was just another of God's assurances that he was born to preach.

Falling in Love

There was a great spiritual awakening on the Frankfort campus the fall Clyde came back for his junior year. Many students became Christians for the first time. Others renewed their commitment to God and became vibrant Christians.

Grace Spencer was one of the students who became a renewed Christian. It was soon after this spiritual awakening on campus that Clyde began to notice Grace in a new way. They had been in class together from the beginning of their freshman year, but she had become a different person after this new commitment. It was as if she was a new girl on campus. She took on a new radiance that everyone noticed, especially Clyde!

Grace and Clyde went together to a Valentine party on a cold, snowy Friday night given in the school dining room. They stood a long time afterward just talking. Clyde felt in his heart when he went to his room that night that this petite, blue eyed blonde with the smiling face would someday be his wife.

Grace Spencer was born of deeply committed Christian parents in Southern Ohio, where her father, a Wesleyan minister, had gone to find work to help get his large family through the depression. She was the fifth of five sisters with one older and one younger brother. She grew up in a parsonage that was scarce on everything but love. Grace recalls, "There was great love and happiness in our home, though we were very poor."

Love grew. By the end of their junior year Clyde and Grace both knew they wanted to spend the rest of their lives together.

There was one snag. They were both still in their teens. Clyde had always been a hard worker. He had a knack for making money and he knew he would have no problem making a living for Grace. She trusted him. They became engaged. They wrote long letters (one was so long Clyde had to send it in two envelopes) back and forth each week during the three months they were apart that summer. When they returned to school in the fall, a June wedding was planned to take place soon after graduation.

June Wedding

It was a simple but beautiful wedding ceremony performed by Grace's father in the small community church where he pastored, on Friday, June 15, 1952. Her sister made her a lovely white brocade dress that was enhanced by the delicate sweetpeas she carried atop a white Bible.

The guest soloist was late in arriving for the wedding ceremony so at the last minute someone else had to be secured to sing the wedding songs. They were not very well sung, but no one seemed to notice because everyone seemed only to see the tall, handsome groom and his beaming bride. Their honeymoon had to be delayed a few days until the factory where Clyde was working closed down for vacation. Then they left for Elizabethtown, Kentucky where Clyde was to conduct a community wide revival in a schoolhouse.

During the day, Clyde would take Grace and they would go knocking on doors inviting people to come to the revival. Each evening they went to the school where Clyde would deliver a fervent message. Many people came forward.

Grace recalls, "When Clyde asked me to marry him, he said, 'Grace, I'm called to be an evangelist. This may mean I will be gone from home. You may have to be alone with our children for long periods of time. Are you still willing to marry me?' 'Yes,' I said, without hesitation, not realizing the seriousness of what he was saying.

"It dawned on me how serious he was about his calling to be an evangelist when every day of our honeymoon was spent inviting people to come to a revival where he was preaching each night. It seemed the right thing to do, though. Only recently did it dawn on me what a strange honeymoon this was, "Grace laughed.

The beauty and some of the depth of this very special love story is obvious to those who know Clyde and Grace. She is still his bride and sweetheart although they've been married more than 38 years. Theirs is a continuing love story, one that grows deeper and richer as the years go by. It is a story that can inspire the lives of all who hear it and take its timeless message of devotion and dedication to heart. It is truly a love story blessed of God.

Super Salesman

5

Super Salesman

After the schoolhouse revival honeymoon in Kentucky, Clyde and Grace returned to their small three-room cottage located on the Frankfort campus. The cottage was furnished with shabby cast-off furniture. Its only nice feature was a screened porch that ran the full length across the front of the cottage. But it was home, their first. Grace was soon able to transform it into a cozy, comfortable place to live.

The brass factory where Clyde had worked the night shift for the past several months closed for a two-week vacation and never reopened because of labor problems. This meant Clyde must look for a new job.

National Homes had a factory in Lafayette, Indiana, which constructed low cost prefabricated houses that were shipped to many parts of the country. Many of the students from the college worked at National Homes. Clyde applied for a job and was hired. He joined the carpool with the other students that left campus each afternoon for their three to eleven night job.

New employees were usually assigned to the glue gun until they could work themselves up to a better and cleaner position. So, Clyde found himself that night gluing the walls together for these pre-fabricated houses. When he returned home about midnight Grace was shocked but amused to see her tall, lanky husband in bluejeans and shirt that were stiff from top to bottom with the messy glue.

In September, Clyde enrolled in a Bible college which was housed on the same campus with the Academy (This college would later become United Wesleyan College). He had been a vital part of the activities on this campus the past four years. He had been an officer of the Student Council and a strong force to keep the activities of the campus Christ centered. But most of these activities would have to be curtailed now because extra time must go toward supporting his new bride and paying his college bills.

One night Clyde came home from his glue gun job, clothes stiff as usual and said, "Grace, there must be a better way to make a living than smearing glue for eight hours a night."

"I agree," she said, "but what kind of work can you get that will leave your mornings free for classes?"

"I'm not sure, but I enjoy selling." Truly, he was gifted as a salesman. In high school he had always been top salesman in any contest he ever entered. He had sold hundreds of boxes of greeting cards. The school yearbook was always a big selling contest on campus. The winner was awarded a trip to Canada one year and Washington, D.C., the next. Clyde won both.

Before he was old enough to be licensed as a salesman, he worked as an insurance solicitor, lining up prospective buyers for another salesman.

Clyde knew he had the ability to sell. He knew in order to be a good salesman you must have faith in the product to be sold. He knew you must work hard and not be easily discouraged. He learned what his assets were. He learned to recognize his failings and to improve them. After searching the want ads in the newspaper, Clyde found an ad that looked like just what he wanted-- "Vacuum Cleaner Salesman Needed." He was interviewed, hired for the job, and assigned a territory in North central Indiana. Clyde was excited with his new job even though it meant driving many miles over snowy road that winter. He soon became top sweeper salesman for the company in spite of the fact he was taking a full load at college.

First Citywide Crusade

The following summer Clyde received an invitation to be the evangelist for a citywide tent crusade in the nearby town of Tipton, Indiana. He knew that nineteen year old college students were not usually extended such an opportunity. He sent word to Ted Sharp, the crusade chairman and a local businessman in Tipton, "I don't think I can accept the invitation because I'm very busy. But I will think and pray about coming for the crusade."

Secretly, Clyde hoped that Mr. Sharp and the committee would go ahead and slate someone else because he felt very incapable.

Grace encouraged him to accept the invitation pointing out that it would be a great opportunity to broaden his ministry.

He accepted.

It proved to be an exciting and challenging ten days. Clyde didn't sell any sweepers during the ten days of the crusade but used the time to study and pray.

Each evening he and Grace with their new baby son, Wesley, drove the twenty-six miles to Tipton.

The crowds that filled the large tent each evening were always in high spirit and were fascinated by the talented Raleigh

Harris; a Quaker who presented a musical program of singing, and he delighted the audience with the unusual talent of playing sleigh bells.

The crowd sat in rapt attention as the tall, six foot four inch young evangelist rose to preach each evening. It was evident from the beginning that Clyde Dupin was a young man who could be trusted. There were no fleshly methods in his ministry It was evident there was something beyond his youthful charisma and natural ability. This young man depended on God. He wanted no glory. He wanted God to have it all.

Much needed refinement and polish in his preaching style would come with time and experience; but for now, no one doubted his humility and sincerity. His love for people was genuine. They responded to the simple message of salvation. Many came forward when the invitation was extended.

Many of the cooperating pastors in the crusade were thrilled with the preaching ability of the budding young evangelist and predicted he would be mightily used of God.

Dr. R.W. Wolfe, Professor of Homiletics, said, "Clyde Dupin was born to preach. He has a rare and unique ability to speak like no other student I have ever had. He has a style of his own and desires to be no one else.

"Clyde is gifted with a unique memory. He can memorize long lists of dates, statistics and the contents of lengthy sermon manuscripts. Since he can memorize his manuscripts easily, he preaches his sermons fluently without notes. This gives him good eye contact and rapport with his audiences."

It was the same summer after this citywide tent crusade that Larry Butts, the state manager for a large insurance company and also a dedicated Christian man, knocked at the door of Clyde and Grace's cottage.

"Hi," Larry said in a cheerful voice, "May I come in?"

"Sure, come in," Clyde invited.

"I hear you are a super salesman," Larry said still in a loud cheery voice. (Clyde learned later that Larry was always loud and cheerful.)

"No, I'm not a super salesman," Clyde answered. "I just have to believe in my product and I work hard."

"Good!" Larry shouted even though he was standing only a few feet from Clyde, "I need an insurance salesman in Elwood, Indiana. This territory has just opened. I want to hire you for this job."

"I'm afraid you will not want me," Clyde said, "because as soon as I finish my theological training I'm going into full time ministry. You probably are looking for a career man."

"No, I'd be happy to have you work for me just until you finish college."

"OK, let me pray about it and talk it over with Grace."

"Good!" Larry shouted as he was going out the door, "I'll pray with you about it, also."

Clyde and Grace talked about the pros and cons of selling insurance. Clyde had enjoyed selling sweepers, but maybe it was time for a change. Maybe God had something better for him. There would be less driving and the pay would be much better. Clyde accepted the job.

He drove to the regional office in Richmond, Indiana, where he would be trained by the District Manager, Herb Sickmeier.

Herb was an enthusiastic Christian man who had received his education at Asbury College and Moody Bible Institute. Clyde enjoyed working with Herb and would continue to work for him the remainder of his college years.

The new job proved to be much more challenging and exciting than any of his previous jobs. He would rush home after his last class, which ended at noon, eat lunch with Grace, grab his briefcase and drive the forty miles to Elwood. There he would talk to prospective buyers about insurance as long as anyone would listen.

Not only did Clyde enjoy the challenge of the new job, but the commission and benefits were good, too. His income took a sharp upturn. It wasn't long until Clyde was sporting a new, shiny Buick loaded with extras. A new brown living room suite replaced the old battered one with faded covers that was furnished with their rented cottage. Anything that Clyde ever undertook to do, whether it was selling garden seeds as a boy, yearbooks for the Bible college, selling sweepers or insurance, he wanted to succeed. He wanted to do his best. He felt God expected it.

There were goals he had his eyes set on in insurance. The President's Club was his first challenge.

To be a member of the President's Club was a coveted honor. But to qualify for membership one must sell seventy-five new policies a month for six months. Clyde became a member of this club in less than six months.

The highest honor the company offered was to be a member of the 600 Club. A diamond was awarded for this. To become a member, one hundred new policies a month for six months must be sold.

Even though Clyde was a full-time college student, he was one of the few to make the 600 Club. Soon he was promoted to assistant district manager. He would continue to sell insurance and train new salesmen in the field.

As Clyde went about selling insurance, he also used these opportunities to share Christ.

One of these opportunities to share Christ was with Irene, a lovely gracious lady, perhaps the wealthiest person in Elwood.

Clyde returned to her house to deliver an insurance

policy she had bought several days before. He knocked on the front door of the big beautiful, stately house.

"Come in," Irene invited, "come in and sit down," pointing to a beautiful brocade over-stuffed chair. Almost before he could be seated in her elegantly furnished livingroom, she said, "Young man, I have thought a lot about your last visit to my home and I enjoyed talking with you. But I have a question I would like to ask you and it is not about insurance."

"Go ahead, ask me," Clyde said smiling.

"You seem so happy. What is the secret?"

Without giving Clyde a chance to answer she continued, "You've probably heard I'm the wealthiest lady in this city. I have hundreds of acres of rich farmland. I have many businesses. I spend my summer in the Palmer House in Chicago. I have a beautiful home in Florida where I spend my winters. I have all this and more, but I'm not happy. I have no peace inside," she pointed to her heart with a hand that sparkled with diamonds.

Irene had not learned the meaning of "What shall it profit a man (or woman) if he shall gain the whole world and lose his soul?" This applies to every individual. Even if he gains all material and social objectives, but loses his soul, all is lost.

"Oh, young man," Irene continued, "just the other night I went to my upstairs bedroom, opened a drawer and pulled out a small automatic pistol. Life is so empty, so empty. I put the gun to my head to take my life. But I just couldn't do it. I just couldn't do it." There were tears in her eyes.

"Young man, what is your secret?" she pleaded.

"Irene," Clyde said, "when I was a nine year old boy, I committed my life to Jesus Christ. I have never gone back on that commitment. Life for me has not always been easy. But I have remained steadfast in my faith in good times and in difficult situations. But God loves us and has a wonderful plan for each of our lives--He so loved us that He gave His only son for us. He loves you and wants to fill your heart with love and peace."

Clyde talked with Irene at great length that evening pointing her to the real source of peace and joy. Tears were running down her face as they prayed together there in Irene's beautiful livingroom.

Those days of college classes, selling insurance and sharing Christ passed quickly.

God's Perfect Will

Northern Indiana had hundreds of beautiful wheat fields. Clyde had passed the golden wheat fields swaying in the soft summer breeze many times as he drove to Elwood. But this last summer he sold insurance it seemed the ripened wheat called out to him--"Behold I say unto you, Lift up your eyes and look on the fields; for they are white already unto harvest." (John 4:35).

Clyde would pull his car over to the side of the road, look out over the wheat fields and with tears streaming down his face he would pray, "Oh, God, bless my ministry. Help me to harvest souls for you."

It was during these times of prayer and struggle beside the road that overlooked the wheat fields when Clyde came to know the perfect will of God for his life. It would be evangelism. This was a great step of faith. It would mean leaving the security of a good paying job to an income that would be very uncertain. But without hesitation he made the decision to follow God's will for his future.

The time had come to enter the full time ministry, the day he had looked forward to since he was a young boy. That same week after Clyde's decision to leave insurance and enter the field of evangelism, late Sunday night, he and Grace were sitting on their front porch. The phone rang. It was Herb calling.

"Hello, Clyde," he began. "I want you to be at the Richmond office in the morning by 9AM. I have great news for you."

"OK, I'll be there," Clyde answered.

He arrived before the 9AM appointment the next morning. Herb was waiting for him.

"Clyde, I have good news," he said enthusiastically. "Larry and I have been discussing you at great length. We have decided you are the kind of person our company needs."

"What do you mean?" Clyde questioned.

"Well, I have a great offer to make you"

"What's that?"

"I'd like for you to stay with me at least one more year. I'll give you a good promotion. You'll be my right hand man. You can make $1,000 a month and still do all the preaching on the weekends that you want to do."

A Difficult Decision

One thousand dollars a month in the fifties was not a bad salary. This was not good news to Clyde. Herb had been a good boss. They had become like brothers and he did not want to hurt him. It was difficult to tell him what he must.

After a long pause (actually he was praying for wisdom), Clyde laid down the pen he had been toying with, took a deep breath and looked Herb straight in the eyes.

"Herb," Clyde said, "I told you when I started working for you it was only a means to help me get my education. My ultimate goal in life is to preach the gospel. These years of selling have been valuable training for me. Perhaps as valuable as my college work; but the time has come for me to move on, to move into full time evangelism. What I'm saying, Herb, is I'm quitting!"

"What do you mean you are quitting?"

"Six weeks from today I will be leaving insurance. And from that day on I plan to devote my time and energies to Christian work."

Herb was stunned.

"What do you plan to start doing six weeks from today?"

"I plan to start conducting revivals and crusades," Clyde answered.

"Do you have very many scheduled?"

"No, I don't have any scheduled," Clyde answered.

"OK, good" Herb said. "You still can work for me. When you have revivals, fine. When you don't, come back here to Richmond and work for me."

"Herb, I know you don't understand and it may sound ridiculous, but God has called me to full time evangelistic work. He wants my full time. I have heard His voice. I know He will open the doors. I don't want any attachment that could distract my full attention and hold me back. I plan for the next six weeks to be the last secular work I ever do. I have a dream, I have a vision, I have a goal, that is to do my best to reach my generation for Christ. I can't give God anything less than the total of my time, talents and future."

As Clyde left the office in mid-afternoon, there was a great peace in his heart that God was going to bless his future. He felt like a school boy who had just turned in his test paper. Deep inside he had the good feeling he had made a good grade. He drove home that day, this verse going over in his mind, "Seek ye first the kingdom of God and his righteousness and all these things shall be added unto you."

On the Road

6

On the Road

"And he saith unto them, Follow me, and I will make you fishers of men. And they straightway left their nets, and followed him " (Matthew 4: 19,20).

Peter and Andrew left their nets by the seashore to follow Jesus. These nets represented their financial security; this was not a sport they engaged in--this was their living!

All who follow Jesus must take a step of faith. Like Peter and Andrew who left their financial security behind, Clyde, too, was leaving his "nets." The future had no financial security except God's promises.

In late summer just before Clyde left the insurance company, Larry called,

"Clyde," he said, "bring Grace and meet me at the Hawthorne Room tonight at 6PM. Herb and our wives will be there, too." (The Hawthorne Room was an exclusive restaurant in Indianapolis.)

It was a lovely going-away party for Clyde. Larry and Herb presented him with a handsome brown leather briefcase and a $500 bonus check.

The $500 was just what Clyde needed to make a down payment on a travel trailer.

What fun and frustration it was to shop for a travel trailer. Grace was always ready to buy the one that was most beautifully decorated even if it was not practical in other ways. Clyde knew it must be small enough for their car to tow easily yet not too small for his family to move about. And, most of all it must not cost too much.

After days of searching, a used, twenty-six foot Palace Ranch Home was settled on. The word, Palace, actually was very deceiving for the trailer was everything but a palace. The outside was a dull chocolate brown with a cream colored stripe painted down the side. Inside there was a tiny kitchen that opened into the eight-foot square living room which also served as the dining room.

The bed consumed most of the space that was allotted to the bedroom. The tiny bathroom was so small that when the door was closed, your backside was against it and your nose was touching the mirror above the sink on the opposite wall.

Clyde was never able to stand erect, because the ceiling was too low; but he felt the trailer was a bargain, so he bought it. Five hundred dollars was paid down and the remaining $1,300 was paid in $35 a month payments.

"Clyde," Grace said with a worried look on her face, "your job ends this week. We only have one revival meeting slated. That one is still a few weeks away. What are we going to do? Where will we go?"

Clyde put his arm gently around her shoulders. "Grace, God has called me to preach evangelistic meetings. He will supply the invitations. I'm not worried," he said.

This was the way it was with Clyde. He always had such great faith. He had learned to obey God, then trust Him to take care of the rest. "Commit thy way unto the Lord; trust, also, in him; and he shall bring it to pass." (Psalm 37:6), "Rest in the Lord and wait patiently." (Psalm 35:7).

It was this practical faith that often amazed Clyde's family and friends. Late the next day good news came from Lexington, Kentucky. Rev. L. S. Houston called on the phone.

"Clyde, I just heard you are going into an evangelistic ministry. One of our campmeeting evangelists has just canceled. Our camp board met and they want you to come and fill in for a few services."

"When does the camp start?" Clyde asked.

"This coming Friday night. Do you have this open?" Rev. Houston questioned.

"I sure do," Clyde almost shouted into the phone, trying not to sound too excited. The truth was all except one ten-day meeting was open. His whole future was open.

Clyde could not keep down the excitement in his voice as he told Grace they would be leaving Thursday for the camp in Kentucky.

Towing a travel trailer was a new experience for Clyde. Except for a few minor problems, things went smoothly until they were descending a long, winding hill just outside of Maysville, Kentucky. The trailer's electrical brakes became overheated because they had to be continually applied to keep the rig from gathering too much momentum down the long hill. They began to smoke and then lost all power.

Clyde knew that without those brakes functioning they were in great danger of gathering such speed he would lose control and they all could be killed.

"Pray, Grace, pray!" Clyde shouted. She didn't have to be asked twice.

"Dear God, save us from an accident. Heal our brakes," she cried. God answered that prayer. Clyde pressed hard on the car brakes until there just wasn't anymore to apply, but the car began to slow and what could have been a serious accident turned into a time of thanksgiving and rejoicing. A tragedy was averted.

The trailer brakes had stopped smoking and were functioning properly again by the time they had arrived safely at the bottom of the next hill.

Grace was elated. She was sure the brakes had been healed. Her faith was not diminished at all when she learned later that the trailer brakes only needed to cool in order to start functioning properly again. That was only the beginning of God's protecting care. The next six years they traveled without any serious accidents. They were hot and tired when they finally pulled their big Buick and travel trailer on to the campground. This was the same campground and the same tabernacle where Clyde had preached the Youth Rally when he was sixteen. He was thrilled to be back.

The entire atmosphere was charged with a spiritual upsurge that seemed to be beaming from every man and woman's face that milled about on the dry, dusty grounds. Even the little children that chased each other in and out among the camp sites and small cottages seemed to radiate the excitement everyone felt.

Nothing had changed. The big white, clapboard tabernacle still dominated the center of the campgrounds. Small white, one-room cottages circled the outskirts of the grounds. Beyond the cottages, back among the trees were campers and tents.

Revivals

This campmeeting turned out to be the miracle that Clyde needed. He was able to slate fourteen revival meetings for the coming year.

The first revival was in a community near Carrolton, Kentucky. Rev. Kenneth George was the pastor who had invited Clyde to this area for a tent meeting. The tent was small, but was filled each evening and many people found Christ.

During the next several months, Clyde preached in many small churches in the states of Kentucky and Indiana. He discovered that too many pastors did little or no preparation for their revival meetings. Because of this, the first few nights were poorly attended. Soon Clyde was preparing his own revival preparation materials along with his own publicity and sending it in advance to the pastors.

Pastor's would ask, "How can I make inroads into my community?"

"You must get out of the four walls of your church," Clyde would urge, "Walk the streets, knock on doors, invite people to church. Get your members doing the same."

God's work will not be effective without prayer, but prayer and works go a long way together. The love offerings were small and they would not always stretch until the next forthcoming pay. So much of those early evangelistic days were lived by faith, faith that God would supply their need.

Faith in God is simply trusting Him enough to step out on that trust. When we step out on this faith, not only does God honor our faith but uses it to reinforce the faith of other Christians.

One of these lessons of stepping out on trust, Clyde recalls, came in February.

They had just closed a revival meeting in Kentucky. The next engagement was over 200 miles away in Terre Haute, Indiana. There simply was not enough money to pay for gas to make the trip and still have money left for groceries.

Grace was taking inventory of their bare refrigerator.

"Clyde, we have no money, we have run out of food, and we need milk for Wesley. What can we do?"

God's Word says in I John 5:14, "And this is the confidence that we have in him that if we ask anything according to his will he heareth us."

So with that in mind, Clyde knelt with Grace beside their bed and prayed, "God, you know we are serving you, our lives are dedicated to your work; we are out of money and it will be seven more days before we are paid again. We need food and milk for our little boy. We ask you to supply our needs. Amen."

No story had ever stirred the faith of Clyde like the story of George Mueller. He had read and reread it. In England, in the year 1836, George Mueller opened his first orphan's home in a single rented building. An unbelieving public was amazed when a second building was opened six months after the first. Mueller concentrated on prayer and the money kept coming in. Eventually there were five new buildings with 110 helpers taking care of 2,020 orphans.

Before opening his first orphanage, Mueller had said that he would consider the experiment of faith and prayer a failure if the orphans ever had to go without food for a single day. They never did.

The answer would come to Clyde and Grace's prayer, though neither had any idea how. It came the next morning. Clyde went to the Post Office to pick up his mail at the General Delivery window. There was a letter from a woman, Ola Langley, who had been a dear friend of Clyde and his family for many years.

When Clyde opened the letter out fell a $10 bill. "Praise the Lord!" Clyde said to the startled people in the Post Office.

The letter went something like this:

"Dear Clyde,
I was awakened out of my sleep a few nights ago. It seemed God told me, 'Send Clyde Dupin that $10 bill you have tucked away.'
'Lord, I have other plans for that $10. Anyway, I can't send it because I don't know where he is,' I argued.
The very next morning I was buying my groceries at Krogers and of all people, who should I meet, your mother. She told me that you were in Terre Haute, Indiana. I needed no further urging from God that I was to send you the $10 bill."

Tears of joy ran down their faces as Clyde and Grace praised God for a marvelous answer to prayer.

But this is not the end. An even stranger thing happened. An insurance salesman called in the home of Ola Langley a few days after she had received a letter back from Clyde thanking her for the $10. The letter was still lying on the coffee table. The religious logo on the front caught the attention of the salesman.

"Who's that letter from?" he asked.

"That's from my preacher boy Clyde Dupin," Ola said. (She still refers to Clyde as her "preacher boy" though he is a grandfather today.)

"Read it." she urged. The salesman opened the letter and began to read. The letter from Clyde told Ola how he and Grace had been praying for a miracle. Her letter with the $10 was the answer. There were tears in the salesman's eyes as he finished the letter.

"Do you mind if I borrow this letter?" he asked.

"Why, no," Ola said in puzzlement, "but why do you want to borrow it?"

"God called me to preach," said the salesman, "but when I graduated from college I didn't enter the ministry."

"Why didn't you?" Ola questioned.

"Because my wife didn't want me to preach. She wanted me to have a job that paid well. She was afraid we would always be poor if we went into the ministry."

"You might be poor," Ola smiled, "but you will never find complete happiness until you obey God."

A few weeks later a radiant salesman returned the borrowed letter to Ola. God had used it to touch the heart of his wife. They both had recommitted their lives to God, and they were making plans to enter full time Christian ministry.

"Seek ye first the kingdom of God and his righteousness and all these things shall be added unto you." (Matthew 6:33)

Crusading
for Christ

7

Crusading for Christ

Clyde logged thousands of miles crisscrossing the country preaching over 300 times that first year in cities and rural, obscure places. Once he preached at Winona Lake in the Billy Sunday Tabernacle to 2,000 young people, yet other times to only a handful in a small primitive church tucked away in the Appalachian Mountains.

Sometimes the audiences were large, sometimes small. One time there was no audience at all.

It was the dead of winter in Indianapolis. The city was gripped by snow and ice. Stinging winds kept the temperature hovering below zero. Clyde arrived Tuesday afternoon at the Nazarene Church. The revival was to start that night.

"I'm sorry," apologized the pastor, "we can not have services tonight. The church furnace is broken. We will start our services tomorrow night."

But the next night the furnace still was not repaired. And so it went the rest of the week; the revival had to be called off. Even though the revival was canceled, the wise pastor saw to it that Clyde was well paid.

The cancellation turned out to be a blessing. It gave Clyde's tired voice and body a much needed rest.

Every church and each pastor had it's own distinct personality. Some were warm and receptive, others were cold and indifferent. Never once did Clyde publicly make a derogatory remark about any pastor. He was always kind and understanding to them.

There were times and occasions that were highly amusing and sometimes very irritating. Clyde always seemed to handle the explosive situations with calmness and wisdom.

He was the guest speaker for a Sunday morning worship in Indianapolis, Indiana. The pastor had taken too much time for his announcements and other preliminaries.

It was fifteen minutes until twelve noon when Clyde arose to preach. He knew there was not enough time to deliver his well prepared sermon. He could see the people were restless and looking at the large-faced clock on the wall. It can be very irritating when a minister uses too much time in unnecessary preliminaries.

"Ladies and gentlemen, just relax. When that clock on the wall says three minutes until twelve, I will stop preaching. No matter where I am in my sermon, I will stop," he laughed.

Being assured they would be dismissed before twelve o'clock noon seemed to relax the audience. They laughed with him, and sat back in their pews to listen intently to the sermon.

With his usual earnestness and sincerity, Clyde preached with a rapid-fire delivery trying to get in as much of the sermon as possible. He glanced at the clock on the wall and it was now five minutes until twelve. He must bring his sermon to a close, he thought; but when he looked again at the clock, to his amazement it still said five minutes until twelve. He preached on, still five minutes until twelve. He finished the sermon. To the surprise and delight of the audience the pastor had unplugged the clock. The service ended with many people coming forward to accept Christ.

Every church Clyde preached in and every audience he preached to, no matter the size, he did his very best. He often said, "If 2 or 2,000 come to hear me preach, I must do my best." He strove constantly to improve his preaching style. He was always learning, reaching forward. He read books, magazines, and newspapers to keep abreast with current affairs. He always had an insatiable desire for knowledge.

Those early years in evangelism Clyde rarely turned down an invitation to preach if he could work it into his schedule. He loved the churches and pastors he worked with, but he had a constant awareness that much more could be accomplished if pastors and churches would just join together for interdenominational crusades.

Of course, he knew Billy Graham was holding great crusades in large cities across the country and around the world, and there were other well known evangelists who conducted citywide crusades, but there were hundreds of smaller towns that had never joined together for a community-wide crusade.

He knew it was time for him to change the old ways of doing things. It was time to re-think, regroup, and to launch out into new and better methods of reaching the lost for Christ.

Dr. Melvin Snyder says, "Clyde has never been willing to just go through the motions; he aims at results--God honors this kind of practical faith."

The Big Tent
Clyde started praying for God to open up a way for him to purchase a tent. He had no money to buy it, but he had faith that God would supply. He recalled the fact that all through the Gospels there kept recurring Jesus' plea for us to have faith, to

ask. "If ye then, being evil, know how to give good gifts unto your children, how much more shall your Father which is in heaven give good things to them that ask him?" (Matthew 7:11)

Faith Rewarded

For what better "thing" could Clyde ask than a tent in which to preach community-wide crusades?

In Wheatland, Indiana, a few weeks after Clyde asked God for the tent, Herb Sickmeier came to hear him speak. After the service that night, Herb was visiting with Clyde and Grace.

"Clyde, have you ever thought about using a tent for community crusades ?"

"Yes, I have. I plan to get one this summer."

"This summer," Clyde said with confidence.

"This summer!" Herb echoed in surprise. "Do you have the money to buy a tent?"

"No, but I have been praying for a tent and I feel sure God will supply it."

"Larry and I have been talking," Herb continued, "and we decided to buy you a tent if you wanted it."

Clyde had never heard more welcome news. He realized now with the tent crusades a reality, he needed to form an association with a board of directors. Clyde wanted to call it the Bible Time Association, after a weekly radio program he had conducted for some months. But some of the board members insisted it be called the Clyde Dupin Evangelistic Association. So, it was.

To help in the advance work for the tent crusades, Clyde secured the services of a college friend, Alfred Case, who was in evangelistic work himself. It was agreed that Alfred would team up with Clyde for the summer crusades, with Paul Hamilton as his soloist and song leader. Alfred, an excellent speaker himself, became a vital part of those crusades.

He and Clyde would take turns preaching in the night services. Alfred, as the advance man, felt a great responsibility for the safety of the tent and the valuable equipment that had to be left in it at night. He felt it should be guarded. So, to the dog pound he went. For one dollar he purchased a big vicious looking dog which he tied to a stake outside the tent. The first night the watchdog escaped and was never seen again. Nothing, however, was ever stolen.

The tent meeting in Stephensburg, Kentucky, a small rural community about 10 miles from where Clyde grew up, was by far the most thrilling crusade the young evangelist had conducted thus far in his ministry. Some nights hundreds of people would pack the tent and over-flow to the outside.

He and a friend, John Langley, would drive the back roads during the day stopping at the houses inviting people to come to the big tent in Stephensburg. School buses were rented to run these back roads. They would be loaded with people when they returned. Night after night Clyde preached the simple gospel, and night after night people came forward.

Hank Jones, one of Stephensburg's notorious drunks and a man who was weathered and sculptured by sin, came to the crusade. Clyde and John had stopped at his house on one of those back roads to invite him and his family to come to the crusade. The small, fragile wife with sad eyes had answered the door.

"No," she said, "we can't come to the tent crusade."

"Why?" Clyde questioned.

"Because me and the kids don't have good clothes."

"That's OK. Come as you are. Bring your husband and come tonight," Clyde urged.

"He works hard all day in the rock quarry. Besides, my husband never goes to church." But her husband with scars across his face, a testimony to the many drunken brawls he had been in, did come to the tent. The sermon struck conviction to his heart; he went forward and accepted Christ.

The community was shocked with unbelief when the word spread, "Old Hank Jones got religion at the tent last night."

Some winked and laughed, "It'll never last."

But it did last. That has been over twenty-five years ago, and Hank Jones became an outstanding lay-minister, winning hundreds of people to Christ.

One hot, sultry July night in 1957, Clyde was conducting a tent crusade in Litchfield, Kentucky, about 15 miles from his own boyhood community.

From the very opening song there was a feeling which permeated the atmosphere that something unusual was about to happen.

It was a service Clyde would never forget. He had preached his best and was giving the invitation when down a side aisle he noticed an older, white haired man was making his way to the front to join the others who had come to accept Christ. It was Clyde's father. Clyde left the platform. He walked down to where his father stood. He put his arm around his father's shoulder and they wept together. Since Clyde was a nine year old boy he had prayed for this night, the night his father would be saved.

The Shepherd

8

The Shepherd

It was Spring, 1959. The Dupin family, Clyde, Grace, Wes, and little Ken, had been crisscrossing the nation in their travel trailer for six years in evangelistic crusades. The next four years on the Dupin calendar were filled with conventions, retreats, Bible conferences, crusades, and camp meetings. God's blessings were evident in Clyde's crusades with hundreds coming to know Christ as their personal Savior.

Yet, there was a gnawing uncertainty during the young evangelists daily prayer time. "It was almost like a sudden vision," Clyde remembers. "God very clearly and definitely told me He wanted me to take a church and serve as a pastor."

"But, Lord." the youthful evangelist pleaded. "I thought you had called me to be an evangelist. I have dedicated my life for the purpose of bringing people to You through these crusades."

After several days in constant prayer, God showed Clyde why He wanted him in the pastorate. Wes, now six years old had never been in public schools and had been taught by his mother through an accredited system for home teaching. Wes needed to be in school for his second grade class. Several other reasons were presented to the evangelist for his tenure as pastor. Clyde had wanted to take some more college classes to help him in his work and as a pastor, he would be able to better understand the relationship of an evangelist to the pastor.

Clyde remembers that a picture of a large, almost empty church in Evansville, Indiana, came to his mind almost everyday during his prayer time. The district superintendent of the Wesleyan Church in Southern Indiana, Rev. Storey, called Clyde one day and tried to interest him in three possible churches which were in need of a pastor. When Clyde heard that Trinity church in Evansville, Indiana, was one of the churches, the young evangelist was elated and promised to pray seriously about the matter.

During a campmeeting at Randleman, North Carolina, in July, 1959, Clyde learned that the District council of the Wesleyan church had voted for him to assume the pastorate at Evansville. However, Dupin received a telegram from someone in the Trinity Church asking him not to come there as pastor. It stated some the church members wanted to recall a former pastor, the founder of the church. Clyde knew God was leading him to be pastor of the Trinity Church so he disregarded the telegram, as a hindrance from Satan, and accepted the pastorate. Dupin found out later that no one in Trinity Church had ever heard of the person whose name had been signed to that telegram.

A Pastor's Heart

The transition from evangelist to pastor was not without problems. After living in a travel trailer for six years, the Dupin's had no furniture to furnish the large brick, four bedroom parsonage adjacent to the church. Clyde had also neglected to ask about the salary and had failed to ask about any staff members in the new church. He soon learned that the situation called for a one-man force.

The first Wednesday evening service, he found no pianist or song leader present among the 22 persons in attendance, which included the four Dupins. Most of the small crowd sat in the back, in one section of the large church, so Clyde, Grace, Wes, and Ken joined them near the back of the sanctuary.

Clyde's first Sunday as pastor of Trinity Wesleyan Church in the fall of 1959 was a new experience for him. There were only 65 persons present for that first Sunday Worship Service, but the young pastor drove home an evangelistic thrust in his first sermon, "If people don't come to church, we will go and bring them in," he preached to the discouraged crowd.

The population of Evansville at the time was about 144,000. The Chrysler corporation had just moved to their new plant in St. Louis and had left many houses vacant throughout the city. But Clyde believed that God had called him to Evansville and that there were many thousands of people in the area that needed to know Christ.

"I want to invite everyone who loves the Lord and wants to see this community won to Christ to meet me at the church on Thursday evening," he announced at the conclusion of his message. On Thursday evening, Clyde left the parsonage early to greet the visitation volunteers at the church. He had planned to begin with a short teaching session and conclude with prayer before he sent the workers out in groups of two each.

At seven-thirty, the first worker arrived, Sunday school superintendent, O. C. Clement, and they chatted while waiting for others to come. After several minutes of waiting, O. C. and

Clyde concluded that no one else was coming. They omitted the teaching session, had prayer and the two of them went out to visit the first families, nearest the church.

The first home visited was Charles and Mary Brooks who welcomed their visit and promised to attend church next Sunday. Sure enough, the Brooks family was present on the following Sunday and they were the first to accept Christ under the new pastorship of Clyde Dupin.

Clyde and O. C. were determined that God wanted them to continue the visitation program even if they had to do it by themselves. But, soon they were joined by others who saw the fruit of faithful visitation. The church began to grow and within nine months, the attendance had swelled to 300 in morning worship. A radio program was conducted on a regular basis during the ten years Clyde served Trinity church.

More than 2,200 professions of faith were witnessed at the church altar during his tenure at Evansville. Attendance continued to increase to as many as 700 during Sunday morning worship. Trinity church had become one of the largest churches in the Wesleyan denomination.

Several other pastors had seen the rapid growth of Trinity church and many asked Clyde why his church was so successful.

"I believe that any church can be successful by following three basic rules," he says. "First, a successful church must be a praying church." During the years that he was at Trinity, he asked the mens group to meet every Saturday evening to pray for the Sunday services. These men, who at first did not want to give up this choice night away from their homes, agreed to do so and soon began to see the rewards of their prayer time with people coming to know Christ.

"Secondly, I believe that a reaching church is necessary for success," he added. The visitation program at Trinity started with O. C. and Clyde but soon increased to nearly 50 regular attenders on Thursday nights.

"I also believe that a successful church must be a loving church, a church where everyone is somebody and can feel loved as brothers and sisters," Clyde insists. Even as the fellowship grew in number, there was always a warm, compassionate love for everyone who entered the doors at Trinity church.

Recently, during a crusade in Haiti, Clyde introduced a special guest at the conclusion of his evening message. With more than 45,000 in attendance that evening, he related the story which took place during the first year of his pastorate in Evansville.

Three doors down the street from Trinity church there was a little house that stood out from the rest on the block. He walked up and boldly knocked at the door and a beautiful young lady with a sad and lonely face answered the door.

"I'm the new pastor at the big church down on the corner," he said. "I've come to talk to you about Christ and the church. Is your husband here?"

"My husband is here, but he doesn't like preachers," she replied.

"But, Ma'am, I want to just talk to your husband"

"He would not want to see you," she insisted.

"But, is he here?" Clyde asked.

"He's around back." Without being invited Clyde walked along the side of the house and around the corner. Seated on the back steps he saw a man under the influence of alcohol. He reached out and took the man's hand.

He let Clyde know that he didn't like preachers. He wasn't kind or gracious, and in language the young pastor understood, he told Clyde that he need not come to his house again.

That couple had six children who had never seen the inside of a church, and they lived only three houses away. The next week, Clyde went back again. Week after week the young pastor visited the home. Sometimes he would find him drunk. Other times he would say unkind things to the pastor.

"He would occasionally come to the parsonage door with his bottle," Clyde says, "but, I loved him. I knew Christ loved him and could save him and make a good man out of him."

For nine months Clyde continued to visit the family on a regular basis. He learned that his neighbor was an alcoholic, that he had been a popular country music entertainer and has written many songs. He had also been on a famous radio program for two years and at one time, had his own television program in Dayton, Ohio. As a teenager, he turned his back on his mother's prayers and went out into the world to make it on his own. But drink had gotten its grip. He'd lost every good job he ever had. He had shamed and abused his precious family. He felt there was no hope but was afraid to die. His health was slowly deteriorating.

One Saturday, there was a timid knock at the study door. The alcoholic's wife opened the door and just barely stepped inside. Troubled and distressed, she looked at Clyde, "Pastor Dupin, I'm ashamed to come. My husband has been so unkind to you, but he is dying and he wants you to come," she related.

Pastor Dupin went immediately to her home and walked into the sickroom. There he saw a man lying on his deathbed, who at one time had stood under the bright lights as a country music star, cheered by his fans. Now he was just a poor drunk whose life was slipping away.

"Brother Dupin, will you pray for me?" he pleaded. "I really need help."

Clyde looked down at the broken, frail piece of humanity and challenged him in a strange way. "Clarence, if God will heal you, will you come to church tomorrow morning?"

"Yes," he replied in a weak voice. The young pastor fell on his knees by the bedside and began to pray. "Oh, God, make this man well. He said he'd come to church if You'd make him well."

As he continued his prayer, he felt Clarence roll out of his bed and kneel at his side. After finishing the prayer Clyde stood up and Clarence also stood up, a well man, and gave the pastor a firm handshake. God had instantly released him. He said it seemed as if a bond of steel had been crushing him to death.

A Miracle

The next night Clarence Williams came to Trinity church and to a place of prayer. He was wonderously saved. Today, he is a preacher of the Gospel and has also written several Gospel songs including "Someday," which was made popular by Doug Oldham, a frequent guest at Trinity Church while Clyde was pastor.

This illustration was given by Clyde at the conclusion of the sermon on a Friday evening of the Haitian crusade. The effect was electric. The crowd cheered as Clarence Williams stood, and hundreds sought the Lord, persuaded that God could also make them a "new creature."

Another important event happened during the Dupin pastorate in Evansville. During the cold Christmas season, a tragic fire in the poor district of Evansville claimed the lives of a mother and four children. A feature newspaper article told the sad story of the father and the surviving children who eventually were turned over to the Family Services in the community.

The Dupins were touched by the tragedy and began to pray, especially for the 18 month old baby girl who was left homeless. They soon felt God wanted them to do more than pray--they would take this little girl into their hearts and home. Clyde went to see his friend, Judge Merrill. He helped Clyde and Grace with the process of adoption, and soon the little girl was theirs.

They named her Joy. "She has been true to her name," Clyde beams about his only daughter. "She has definitely brought joy to our house and continues to do so even today."

During the ten years that Clyde pastored not only did he work long and hard for his church, but he gave many hours to promote the good of the whole community. He was a member of the Youth for Christ board, President of the Evansville Ministerial Association, spoke for many civic activities and worked hard for the spiritual upbuilding of the whole community.

Even though Clyde was a busy pastor, he felt he must not neglect his own family. He set aside Tuesday as family day. Clyde and Grace always tried to make Tuesday a very special day with their children. Sometimes it might be a picnic in the park or the whole family exploring back, out-of-the way places on their bicycles. Sometimes on a cold, snowy, winter Tuesday night they would all bundle up, drive to the West side of Evansville where there were hills and go snow sledding. Then they would come home cold, tired and happy to drink hot chocolate with fresh donuts.

Wesley the oldest son of Clyde and Grace said, "Dad always had time for us kids. Even though Dad was a busy man and had many demands on his time while in the pastorate, we never hesitated to talk to him about our problems. He always had time to pray and counsel with each of us children individually.

"Our family worship each evening was not only a time of praise and thanksgiving, but a time when we prayed about our problems," Wesley added.

"I remember," Wes continued, "walking with Dad and Ken on the fairways during an occasional golf game. Dad would talk to us about a wonderful plan God had for each of our lives. All my life I felt God wanted me to work with my Dad in the ministry."

Even today no one can be with Wesley very long until he senses the great love and admiration he has for his father.

The years in Evansville were exciting and happy years. The church people loved and respected their young pastor and often would vote to raise Clyde's pay. There were times he would refuse to accept a raise, insisting the money be used to expand the ministry of the church.

Even though the church had unanimously voted a lifetime pastorship for Clyde and he would have been happy to have stayed at the Evansville church for a lifetime, he knew deep in his heart that God had other plans.

'Which Door, Lord?'

9

"Which Door, Lord?"

For several years at Evansville, Clyde had dreamed and prayed for a city-wide crusade in his city. As president of the ministerial association, he was interested in bringing Dr.Ford Philpot to lead the joint venture sponsored by the Evansville churches.

However, when a delegation of pastors met in Clyde's study, the name of Bill Glass, a very successful evangelist and an all-pro football player was suggested. After much prayer and discussion, Glass was invited to come to conduct the crusade.

Several months before the Evansville Crusade, Bill Glass' crusade director, Bill Carlson, was seated across the desk in Clyde's study. He started by saying, "Clyde, Bill Glass and I have been looking for a man like you all across the country."

"What do you mean?" Dupin said.

"Well," Carlson continued, "this is confidential. Bill Glass is planning to retire from professional football next year and give full time to crusade evangelism. We need you on our team."

"Hey, Carlson, you are talking to a very happy pastor. I have a very exciting ministry here at Trinity Church," Clyde said emphatically.

"I know, I know," Carlson smiled, "that is the reason Glass and I want you--because you are a success. We have been praying and we feel you are the man for our team. Your experience in evangelism, organizational ability, and success as a pastor makes you the very man we need."

"I'm not interested, but I will pray about the offer," Clyde promised, thinking that would be the end of that matter. A few days passed and Clyde continued to pray about the Bill Glass offer but did not give it any serious consideration

To make matters more complicated, he was interrupted one morning in his study by a phone call from the chairman of the board at his former alma mater, United Wesleyan College. Rev. Felsburg was calling to ask him to consider the presidency of the college. The board had met and was seriously considering him as their next president. He promised to pray about it but after another call Clyde had to admit that he felt no definite leading of the Lord to pursue this open door. He graciously thanked them for their support and consideration but declined the offer. Yet, he knew that God was beginning to bring about circumstances for a major move.

During the first week of September, 1968, Pastor Dupin was given a scholarship to attend the Billy Graham School of Evangelism in conjunction with the crusade in Pittsburgh. The school was electrifying and inspirational as the crusade continued to build each night. One evening while alone in his hotel room, Clyde was emotionally moved by the presence of the Holy Spirit. He had learned many years before to listen to that still, small voice as it spoke to him.

"Son, I want you to return to the field of evangelism."

"Lord," Clyde replied with tears now coarsing down his cheeks.

"I'm willing to do what you want. But, what would you have me to do?"

After staying on his knees for a long time, Clyde asked God to open some specific door during the month of September if it was His desire to return to evangelism on a full-time basis. If there were no specific offers during the next three weeks, he would consider that the enthusiasm of the Billy Graham crusade was intended to make him a more evangelistic pastor and he was ready to return to his church and use the many things he had learned to become a more effective pastor.

On the Road, Again

Yet, he knew deep in his heart that this was a special visitation of the Holy Spirit. After returning home from Pittsburgh, he said nothing to Grace about the hotel room incident. On Monday morning, after the children had gone to school, he remained at home, rather than rush off to his study, as was his custom. He asked Grace to sit down by him on the couch.

"Dear," he said slowly. "I have something to tell you."

Tears streamed down her cheeks as she said, "Honey, You don't have to tell me anything. One morning while you were in Pittsburgh, I was standing at the sink doing the breakfast dishes," she related. "God spoke to me as I prayed. I have already made my commitment and I know that I will have to give you up to evangelism," she added.

Clyde put his big arms around her small body and they rededicated their lives anew to His leading. Two weeks had passed and there were no specific doors opened for Clyde's evangelistic ministry. The last day of September arrived and he was ready to begin the Sunday morning service at Trinity when Wes came into his study.

"Dad," he said excitingly. "Did you know that Dr. Wesley Lovin from our denominational headquarters is here at our church this morning?"

"No," Clyde replied. "I haven't had time to greet any of our visitors yet."

After the morning worship, Clyde stood at the door as the worshippers were leaving. He greeted Dr. and Mrs. Lovin and invited them to have lunch with the Dupins. During the afternoon, when they sat down to talk, the denominational executive became serious.

"Clyde, I might as well tell you why I am here," he began. "We are planning to open a new department in our church and the general board has authorized me to ask if you would be interested in serving as our new secretary for evangelism for the Wesleyan Church."

The young pastor was stunned, shocked! This was the last day of September and Clyde had asked God to·open some specific door before the end of the month. Perhaps this was what God had in mind all the time. At the same time, Bill Carlson had called and revived the possibilities of a working relationship with the Bill Glass crusades. Two specific invitations had come the same day on the last day of the month. Clyde could only promise that he would pray about both situations and let God do the leading.

Within the next few days, Clyde visited the denominational headquarters and talked with several of their leaders. He was greatly impressed and inspired but did not feel that this was what God wanted. He thanked them for their gracious and kind invitation.

He also spent a few days with Bill Glass in trying to determine God's leadership.

"I was greatly impressed with Bill Glass," he said. "His maturity and sincerity for the Word of God and Evangelism were magnetic, but, I was still unsure about God's leadership."

Several weeks passed as Clyde and Grace continued to pray about the matter. In February, they attended a joint service in another church and heard a visiting minister preach on Luke 18:29-30. As he read, "Verily I say unto you, there is no man that hath left house, or parents, or brethren, or wife, or children, for the kingdom of God's sake, who shall not receive manifold more in this present time, and in the world to come life everlasting,"

Clyde knew this was it. The scriptures spoke directly to both Clyde and Grace. They nudged each other almost simultaneously. Both of them knew in their hearts that they would go with the Bill Glass organization. It was sealed that day. When Bill called Clyde, he related that he felt that God was definitely leading him to join the Bill Glass team, and that he was ready to make the move as soon as possible.

Clyde agreed to resign his church the next Sunday morning. With tears in his eyes and a loving heart he told his sad congregation that God was leading him into full time evangelism. He expressed his love to them and thanked them for their loyal support during the ten years he served "the best people in the world" as their pastor.

Clyde always believed that he was born to be an evangelist. But, he thanked God that He was given the privilege of being a pastor and the opportunity of being with his family during the formative years of his children. Wes was now a junior in high school and Ken had grown into his teen age years. The whole family became extremely excited about the new opportunities in the field of evangelism. But, there were many hurdles to overcome as they made their final plans to join the Bill Glass association

Bill Glass Crusades

10

Bill Glass Crusades

Now that God's leadership had been firmly planted in their minds, the Dupin family set out to tackle the multiple problems in leaving their beloved church and entering into full-time evangelism with the Bill Glass organization. They stayed at the church for an additional 90-days, while a new pastor was being sought. The Dupins last Sunday at Trinity church was very emotional for the whole congregation as well as their immediate family.

"These people were very near and dear to my heart," Clyde says. "I had brought many of them to the Lord and had watched them mature into strong, gracious Christians. It was very hard for me to leave these wonderful people, but I knew that God had other plans for my life and I would not disappoint Him."

Clyde and Grace had never owned a home of their own. When they first married they lived in a small cottage on the college campus and then in a travel trailer. From this very small travel trailer they moved into the parsonage at Trinity Church. Now that Clyde would be traveling with Bill Glass they must move out of the parsonage into their own house. They had an attractive tri-level house built in Melody Hills near the Evansville airport where Clyde would be flying in and out frequently.

Enthused by his new challenge, Clyde delved into his work as crusade director for the Bill Glass Evangelistic Association. He was selected as vice president and served on the board of directors, a position he continues to hold today.

In his new job, he was responsible for the directing of interdenominational crusades in major cities throughout the nation. He trained more than 12,000 counselors and spoke to numerous pastor's conferences, civic clubs, and pre-crusade rallies. Clyde worked very closely with Bill Carlson and Bill Glass and was exposed to several prominent religious leaders and professional Christian athletes.

"I had always admired Bill Glass as an outstanding pro-football, defensive end for the Cleveland Browns," Clyde says. "But, most of all I admire him for his firm Christian stand."

Before his retirement from professional football in 1969, Bill Glass was known as an evangelist in headgear and shoulder pads. John Underwood, writer for *Sports Illustrated*, said, "Bill Glass had been known to raise knots on halfbacks on Sunday afternoon and goose pimples on his congregations on Sunday night."

Organizing Crusades

Clyde's first assignment was to set up the arrangements for a great crusade at Topeka, Kansas. He drew on his experience of his pre-pastorate days and also had the benefit of working with Bill Carlson, a former Air Force instructor who had broad experience in crusade planning.

The Topeka crusade was an overwhelming success and hundreds came to know the Lord as their Savior. Clyde, who had always had an evangelistic heart, was thrilled at the sight of hundreds coming to acknowledge Christ as Lord each evening. He knew this was where God wanted him to serve and that for the present, he was in the Lord's will.

The schedule was hectic at times. One night, at Findlay, Ohio, Bill Glass and Clyde left for Toledo where they caught a plane to Dallas. There, they boarded a little Texas International plane for a bumpy flight to Artesia, New Mexico, to meet with a group who had invited them for a crusade. The flight was nauseating to say the least. Both of the evangelists had been tossed and thrown in the turbulent plane. After what seemed to be several hours, the little plane landed safely at the Artesia airport.

"Bill, there is a large reception line waiting outside the plane," Clyde said as he looked out the window. "Wouldn't you know it," Bill replied, "just when we both look a mess."

Clyde volunteered to go ahead while Bill took a few minutes to comb his hair and straighten himself. It was a little uncommon for a welcoming committee from the Chamber of Commerce to greet evangelists, but Bill had been honored with the "key to the city" in several places during his pro-football days.

"Hi. I'm Clyde Dupin, crusade director for Bill Glass," he introduced himself as he made his way down the line, shaking hands with each member of the welcoming committee.

"Bill will be here in a moment," he explained to each of them as he pumped their hands. The cordial group smiled as they continued to glance toward the plane door. To their surprise and embarrassment, they soon learned that the welcoming committee from the Chamber of Commerce had not come to meet them, but another dignitary on the same flight.

"Well," Clyde remarked. "At least, I got acquainted with most of them and they all know that Bill Glass is in town," Clyde said sheepishly.

Grace said, "When Clyde started traveling with Bill Glass, I missed having him at home every night. But I knew God had called Clyde into this new ministry with Glass. Even though I was lonely at times, still I found peace and happiness in remaining at home taking care of our children. I increased my studies at Indiana State University, read more, and prayed more for my plane-hopping husband in his evangelistic endeavors. There is contentment in knowing you are in God's will."

The tri-level house in Melody Hills was home to the Dupins for three years. Then in June, 1972, the moving van backed up to the door of their house. Again, they would move. This time to Kernersville, North Carolina, where Ken had been attending a Christian academy. The Dupins, also, wanted their youngest child, Joy, to attend this same school, since Clyde's work often took him to the North Carolina area and Grace had been offered a job teaching art at the academy where the children would be attending. They were sure God was directing this move. They look back eight years later and say, "We know this move was a good one."

Since his retirement from pro-football, the Bill Glass crusades took on new dimensions. From Indianapolis, to Lexington, from Madison, Wisconsin, to Bakersfield, California, from Huron, South Dakota, to Americus, Georgia, the city-wide crusades were held in coliseums and football stadiums with thousands of persons coming to know Christ.

Clyde was in the middle of the activity and was thrilled as he saw the hundreds of counselors he had personally trained, leading inquirers into a personal relationship with Jesus Christ.

Working with Bill and his team was most rewarding and satisfying, but after five years, he believed that God was again moving him into another area of His plan.

"Bill Glass is one of the finest men I know," Clyde admits. "In all the years I had worked with him, there was never an unkind word, never a harsh remark between us."

Clyde talked confidentially with Bill on several occasions and shared with him the deep burden that God had given him to form his own evangelistic team. Bill was most sympathetic and asked Clyde to pray a little longer for God's perfect will. He also offered to help Clyde set up his own staff and become an associate evangelist on the Bill Glass team, with special emphasis on the hundreds of smaller towns desiring county-wide crusades.

As Clyde continued to pray, he felt a definite leading to form his own, independent organization and gave Bill a six months notice before leaving. Clyde took special interest in training his replacement, Dick Rohrer, a former Youth for Christ staff member, before resigning in 1974.

"I always felt that God brought Bill and me together," Dupin believes. "First of all, I have no greater friend than Bill Glass. Secondly, it was through his organization that I learned in-depth crusade strategy and follow-up, both of which are so necessary for effective evangelism."

During his last year with the organization, Clyde had surgery in a Winston-Salem hospital. It was during this specific time that God spoke clearly to him about the Clyde Dupin Ministries. While recuperating, he read several books on prayer, which greatly enhanced his prayer life. At the same time, Grace had devoured a book by E. Stanley Jones which greatly altered her prayer life. They both began to pray in a new way. Grace, inspired by her new found blessing, began to share with other women. Today, she leads prayer teas during the crusades and in some cities has had as many as 1,000 women meeting to pray for the crusades.

Clyde's time in the hospital was spent in reflection and devotion to God. Now 41, he believed that the Lord was leading him into the greatest, most productive time of his life. The security of his position with the Bill Glass organization would be forfeited, he would be stepping out into an unknown venture, but, he was assured that God was leading. That made all the difference in the world to the man who believed he was born to be an evangelist.

Expect a
Miracle

11

Expect a Miracle

Clyde Dupin has never been afraid of a challenge. One verse that he lives by is, "I can do all things through Christ which strengtheneth me." (Philippians 4:13).

Clyde says, "I have always liked a challenge, I like to work, always have. I plan, dream, organize, and look ahead. God has given me goals, and I hold these goals tenaciously in my mind and bathe them in prayer until by the process of mental osmosis they seep deep into my unconscious. I've always been driven by the urge to do jobs well and never hesitated to tackle new ones. Why? Just because God made me that way. I'm glad He did! I know none of these dreams can be realized without the Holy Spirit working in me."

This really describes Clyde's whole life. It was the reason for the challenge that came to him next. It was with this same sense of direction, the direction of the Holy Spirit, that Clyde left Bill Glass and would reorganize the Clyde Dupin Evangelistic Association, Inc., which had been dissolved when he became a pastor. Even Bill Glass had sensed that God might someday use Clyde Dupin in a greater way. Several times he had said, "Clyde, I fear someday you will leave my organization, and I would certainly hate to see your go. You are a gifted evangelist and could have a tremendous ministry on your own."

Forming the Board

Bill's prophetic words were fulfilled. In November, 1974, Clyde had invited fifteen of his most trusted and loyal friends including his pastor, Dr. Clyde Parker, and former board members, Larry Butts, and Herb Sickmeier, to meet in Gatlinburg, Tennessee, to organize the Clyde Dupin Ministries.

These men knew Clyde had been endowed with humility, sincerity, and the natural ability to be an evangelist. They also knew the primary reason for his past successes was the power of God behind him. Clyde's faith was magnetic and contagious. His compassion for lost souls was genuine. This organizational meeting in Gatlinburg took on a revival atmosphere as Clyde challenged the newly formed board to "Expect A Miracle."

Bob Brennen, a former Big Ten Track Coach at the University of Wisconsin and a dedicated Lutheran layman, was chosen as Chairman of the Board. Russell Roberts, a United Methodist layman and John Deere dealer in Lebanon, Indiana, served as Vice Chairman. A life-long friend and a Nazarene layman, Ed Johnson, from Indianapolis, Indiana, was the efficient Secretary of the Board. The Treasurer of the organization, Dr. Wesley Phillips, is Clyde's personal physician and fellow church member.

"These board members are a vital part of my ministry," Clyde says. "They are my greatest prayer support, and give guidance to my ministry. These men, along with some personal friends, pay me a modest salary. I never accept love offerings from crusades."

Clyde told his board that he did not want a large organization but only enough staff people to help him fulfill his mission in evangelism.

Wesley Dupin

Wesley, Clyde's oldest son, who had recently graduated from college, became his first Crusade Director. He would work with local committees in preparation for city-wide crusades and direct the music program. Many minister friends welcomed the news that Clyde would again be available for city-wide crusades. Some of these ministers he had worked with years ago in evangelism helped initiate invitations.

Almost immediately more invitations were received for city-wide crusades than could be accepted. First, a small three-room apartment was rented for office space, but this was soon outgrown, and the Clyde Dupin Ministries was moved to a six-room, red brick house on one of the main streets of the quaint little town of Kernersville, North Carolina, just .

An important aspect of the office is the secretary. It would be difficult to find a secretary who works harder and is more dedicated than Sharon Oyler. She kept the office running smoothly even though Clyde Dupin is away many days at a time. Sharon is a woman of prayer who moves with the philosophy that her work is a special ministry.

A special room, perhaps the most important one in the entire office, is Clyde's prayer room. Many prayer promises, such as "Call unto me and I will answer thee and show thee great and mighty things which thou knowest not." (Jeremiah 33:3), are printed in bold letters and hang on the wall behind the altar in this prayer room. These remind Clyde that he serves a great God who can answer fervent prayer.

On this altar are hundreds of letters--letters from brokenhearted people, lonely people, sick people, wayward children, confused and mixed up people.

One of these was a pathetic letter from a 16 year old high school girl in Wilkes-Barre, Pennsylvania, where Clyde held a crusade. She had come forward in the crusade and accepted Christ. Her problem:

"Dear Rev. Dupin,
I have been the only girl member in a vicious
street gang with 12 boys. I was the sex partner
to all 12 of these boys. How can I find strength
and courage to go on alone and never return
to this old life?"

This traumatic experience preyed on the girl's mind. She knew God had forgiven her for these terrible sins, but she needed help. Clyde not only prayed for this teenage girl but he wrote her a personal letter directing her to the pastor of a Bible believing church in her area.

Clyde takes each of these hundreds of prayer requests he receives seriously. Not only does he pray about them but many letters receive a personal answer. His love and compassion for people is genuine. Those who know him best feel this is one of the reasons why God has been able to use him in such an effective way.

Others criticize him for giving too much time to the needs of a common, ordinary people. In 1975, the Wesleyan Church made plans to launch an international radio program, "The Wesleyan Hour." The Walter F. Bennett Company would be the marketing agency for this program. Every member of the radio commission agreed that this endeavor required a talented and colorful speaker, one who could capture the attention of a vast secular audience.

If a minister is successful in one pulpit, or evangelism or whatever field of work he is in, there are always other doors opening to him. This had always been true in Dupin's life. So the church looked to him again.

Dr. Wesley Lovin, Secretary of Church Extension and head of Radio Commission, called Clyde Dupin from Marion, Indiana to make an appointment to meet with him in Kernersville, North Carolina.

"I have something very important to talk with you about," Dr. Lovin had said.

When Dr. Lovin arrived in Kernersville he got right to the reason for his visit. "Clyde," he said, "the denomination is going on international radio. Eventually we plan to be on hundreds of stations around the world. It is a marvelous opportunity to spread the Gospel. We have considered several outstanding speakers but the Radio Commission unanimously voted that you be the 'Wesleyan Hour' speaker. Will you consider it?"

"Of course, I'll consider it," Dupin said. "I feel very honored and humbled by this offer, but I will have to pray and ask God's direction."

Whenever an opportunity of this magnitude came to Clyde his first thought was, "Why me, Lord? I'm often amazed that God has chosen to use me, being just an insignificant country boy."

Clyde Dupin took this offer seriously and prayed about it for many days. He turned to his closest confidante and prayer partner, Grace, for advice and counsel. They fasted and prayed together for the answer. Many of his closest friends advised him to accept the offer which, they said, may only come once in a lifetime..

"I was tempted," Clyde said, "to accept this offer because of the vastness of the audience that could be reached through the electronic media; but my final decision had to be no.

"A ministry of that magnitude," Clyde relates, "might soon require more time than I would be able to devote to it. My major ministry is interdenominational crusades. I felt a denominational radio program might cause some conflict of interest."

Clyde recommended a close friend, Norman Wilson, a highly qualified minister, to be the radio program's speaker. He was chosen.

"Each time I hear 'The Wesleyan Hour,'" Dupin said, "I know Norm Wilson was God's choice for this program. He is one of America's greatest radio speakers."

A media that Clyde Dupin did turn to soon after he turned down the speaker for the radio program was the newspaper. The news media is a powerful tool, a tool that is not monopolized enough by the church world.

Clyde felt God was leading him to write a newspaper column, entitled "Religious Viewpoint." This column has grown in popularity and is now carried in about 50 newspapers across the nation.

It seems that God has always blessed Clyde Dupin in every ministry in which he has served. Dupin says all his life he has operated by Philippians 4:13, "I can do all things through Christ which strengtheneth me." He quotes this passage when a challenge appears too great, when problems seem to have no solution, or when he is bone tired and it seems he cannot go on.

The year 1978 marked the 25th year for Clyde Dupin in full time ministry. This was celebrated at the annual board meeting in Gatlinburg, Tennessee, by the board members. The celebration was a total surprise to Clyde. It had been spearheaded by his son, Wesley, and board Chairman, Bob Brennan.

After a delicious banquet meal was served, a delightful program was presented highlighting Dupin's 25 years in the ministry. Telegrams and letters of congratulation were read from friends far and near. Some of those who sent messages were Bill Glass, Oral Roberts, Roy Rogers and Dale Evans, Doug Oldham, Leighton Ford, and many church leaders.

Dupin's past 25 years of ministry was portrayed in an exciting slide presentation. All those present were awed and blessed to see the miracles that God had wrought through Clyde Dupin's ministry. Clyde himself was moved to tears as he watched the presentation.

"After the celebrating was over that night," Dupin exclaimed, "I went to my room and fell on my knees to thank God for the past 25 years of spreading the gospel. I have no doubt the Second Coming of Christ is near at hand. I must get the gospel out now. I plan to spend the next 25 years preaching the simple gospel of John 3:16: 'For God so loved the world that he gave his only begotten son, that whosoever believeth in him should not perish but have everlasting life.'"

This, truly, is the greatest miracle of them all!

PHOTO SECTION

Clyde Dupin Birthplace. East view, Kentucky. Febuary 22, 1933.

Mother & Dad Dupin.

Three brothers; Clyde, 5; Clayton, 8; and Cecil, 10.

(Left) The Boy Preacher

(Below) High School Graduation

(Below) Teenagers-Clyde and Grace

(Right) The Wedding, June 15, 1951.

A tent Crusade near Clyde Dupin's boyhood home, 1954.

(Above) the Clyde Dupin tent overflows.

(Right) Clyde Dupin and song leader Paul Hamilton were teamates from 1955 to 1959.

Clyde and Grace and their family, Ken, Joy, and Wes; 1967

Clyde pastored Trinity Church, Evansville, Indiana, from 1959 to 1969

The Board of Clyde Dupin Ministries, Inc. (Standing) Dick Gerber, Jerry Snyder, Dale Hileman, Larry Butts, Ed Johnson, Harold Treece, James Rice, George Joslin, Clyde Parker. (Seated) Wesley Phillips, Herb Sickmeier, Wes Dupin, Clyde Dupin, Bob Brennan, Laverne Mohl, Russell Roberts; 1976.

(Above) Clyde Dupin at his office in Kernersville, N.C.

(Right) Clyde & Grace Dupin at a crusade.

(Left) Clyde Dupin at 47 has preached face to face to one and one-half million souls.

(above) At home, Clyde, Joy and Grace; 1975

Clyde and Grace, Bluffton Indiana Crusade; 1978

(Left) Clyde Dupin and Dr. AdrianRogers, President of Southern Baptist Convention; 1979

(Below) Second Row: Grace and Clyde Dupin-platform guest at Billy Graham's Nashville Crusade; 1979

(Above) Clyde Dupin and Norm Palmer, former golf pro for President Eisenhower.

(Right) Clyde Dupin and crusade organist, John Innes.

Two hundred churches participate in Clyde Dupin Crusade, Barbados, W.I.,1978.

Clyde Dupin and Bill Glass, 1973.

Father and Son-- Evangelist Clyde Dupin and Song Leader Wes Dupin.

(Above) A typical Clyde Dupin Crusade --4000 at Rutherford-ton, NC, 1978.

(Right) Clyde Dupin Team: Bob Anderson, Hoover Smith, Ken Dupin, Wes Dupin, Grace Dupin.

(Above) Clyde Dupin, President of Haitian Parliament and Roney Gilot, Secretary of State, at crusade.

(Left) As Dr. Claude Noel interprets, Clyde Dupin watches 300 respond to the invitation.

In Port-au-Prince, Haiti, 1979, 45,000 hear Clyde Dupin in Soccer Stadium.

Clyde, sharing the Word at a Crusade.

Clyde, Grace:
An evening at home

Clyde and Grace with
Haitian Crusade Team, 1983

At 47, Clyde Dupin belives the past is only a prelude to greater victories.

Work of
an Evangelist

12

Work of an Evangelist

Many casual observers think the life of an evangelist is a glamorous, fun-filled, exciting time, with little responsibility except to preach a 35 minute sermon each evening and enjoy several hours of leisure during the days. They may not be aware that the crusade in their community started more than nine months before when the staff member from the Clyde Dupin Crusade met with local pastors and began to put the needed committees and workers together for a successful crusade.

An office is established in each town or city where a crusade is to be held and four or five days are spent each month by a staff member preceding the crusade in coordinating the various committees. Advertising is begun and counselors are trained. The local finance committee goes to work early to raise the needed budget. Preparation is made for follow-up on those making decisions during the crusade. Every new Christian is assigned a counselor on a one-to-one basis for five weeks after each crusade with emphasis toward joining one of the participating churches for active fellowship.

"I believe in the local church," Clyde preaches. "A new Christian needs the fellowship of other Christians, if he is to mature in his new found life."

Newspaper Interview

Recently, in Corydon, a small county-seat town of 3,000 population in Southern Indiana, a reporter for the Corydon Democrat followed the evangelist for an in-depth report for his newspaper. Randy West, the reporter, filed this first-hand account, after spending a day with the evangelist.

"Clyde Dupin, the earnest evangelist in the threepiece suit, holds his big Bible aloft and calls 1,600 souls to come forward and make a decision for Christ. Clyde Dupin, the small-town Billy Graham, who brings a simple Gospel message of salvation to Harrison County's biggest revival ever...Is he the same man the next morning? Yes!

"The Reverend Clyde Dupin, 47, is an evangelist morning, noon, and night. He's a 24-hour-a-day witness. Each morning, as soon as he wakes up, he meditates on a couple of pre-selected scripture passages and then he catches the latest news on TV.

"Before eating his customarily small breakfast -- it was a Danish pastry last Wednesday morning at the Old Capitol Inn -- Dupin offers a short prayer.

"What does it take to be an evangelist? 'First of all,' he answers quickly, 'it takes total integrity.' It also requires sincerity, a good understanding of various denominations and their unique customs, organization, and financial accountability to a board of directors as well as the community where he's preaching.

"One learns soon that he also believes strongly in discipline and in prayer as a source of strength. Dupin is an interdenominational evangelist who lives in Kernersville, N. C., not far from Winston Salem. At age nine he saw his first revival in a tent, and not long afterwards he had read the entire Bible. He started his career as a boy preacher of the Gospel in the hills of Kentucky, near Elizabethtown.

"Last Wednesday morning, he was well aware of a chilling movie shown the night before on TV. 'Guyana Tragedy' dramatized the grisly story of the Rev. Jim Jones, a charismatic madman who ordered his frightened flock to commit mass suicide at Jonestown.

"Being an evangelist isn't easy. 'The most difficult thing is constantly having to prove yourself.' he says. Evangelism has been stained by some evangelists and pastors in many communities who have 'gone astray' and brought reproach to Jesus Christ. People tend to classify evangelists together more than pastors, teachers or lawyers.

"'That's a little cross that I have to bear, and I'm willing to do it for the sake of Jesus,' he says.

"As Dupin finished his Danish, his oldest son, Wes, and John Innes, a charming Britisher, show up for breakfast. Wes is crusade director, and John works as organist for both Dupin and the Billy Graham Crusades. Although they often work crusades together, the two talk excitingly, as if they haven't seen each other for years.

"Dupin and his son head for a radio interview at WJDW, and they're a bit late. As they drive into Corydon in a car provided by a local dealer for the eight-day crusade, they pass a large orange billboard proclaiming the 'Harrison County Clyde Dupin Reachout Crusade' each night of the week (starting at 7:27 p.m., which no one forgets).

"Dupin's smiling face beams from the billboard. Dupin says he loves his work and is committed to evangelism, but he admits that he does not like the vast amounts of publicity required to provoke interest and draw big crowds. At the radio station, Jon Walsh interviews Dupin and declares him a talk show host's dream because he doesn't answer with 'Yes' or 'No.'

"When Dupin answers a question, the schedule and commercials are forgotten. He takes a few calls--some of the callers are real talkers, too-- and at one point he mentions the 'awesome responsibility of staring into the faces of hundreds of young people' the night before at the Youth Night.

"Leaving the station, he talks at length to several young women in the office about their faith. To check on the number of decisions made at the revival Tuesday night, Wes and his father head for the crusade headquarters at the late Dr. Sam Martin's office. During the drive through Corydon, they talk about 'planting the seed of harvests' they hope local ministers will reap later.

"No one's at the crusade office --the secretary, Nancy Jackson, is attending a 'Ladies Prayer Tea' conducted by Grace Dupin, Clyde's wife of almost 29 years. They look over the decision cards and they're pleased: 91 were made Tuesday night.

"The decisions represent people from at least 20 county churches. Why do they emphasize public decisions? 'This is just an opportunity to make a decision for Christ,' Dupin says. 'Skeptics look at it as a response to you (the evangelist), not God. They don't think about the counseling that follows. It takes a lot of courage to do it. You've got to have something inside.'

"Following the crusade, local people conduct a five-week follow-up program. 'We try to conserve the results of the crusade,' Dupin says. 'A lot of people don't know this. We want them to become part of their local churches.'

Back at the motel, Clyde and Wes join Innes for their regular morning meeting. They cover a lot of ground. Program details. Family anecdotes. The differences between Billy Graham and impostors like Jim Jones (those who are not of God will come to naught, Dupin says). Problems with children their wives have told them about on the telephone. People at the crusade who have asked for prayers. And Suzanne Johnson. She is a lovely singer who testified the night before about her family's unexpected financial disaster.

"And then, following their daily custom, each falls to his knees and puts his head in a chair or sofa. In turn, each prays aloud, earnestly, eagerly, and at length. Almost everything in their rambling and interesting conversation of a moment ago is prayed about, with great intensity. For 10 or 15 minutes, the three pray. They spill out their concerns, their tears, and their hopes. They ask for help and guidance and especially strength.

"Then they all get up, obviously refreshed, and continue to talk in an animated, loving manner. They enjoy each others' company.

"Grace Dupin appears and joins her husband for lunch. She has just finished another 'Ladies Prayer Tea' at the Old Capitol United Methodist Church. Men aren't invited. She talks about things like the 'The Beautiful Woman,' 'Power and Poise,' and 'Bloom Where you're Planted.' On Monday she spoke to 98 women. The next day 130 are there, and then 189 and then 203.

"After lunch, the couple head out for their daily walk to get some much-needed exercise. 'I do it religiously,' Clyde says. They like to cover one or two miles each day. She prefers to jog, but a back problem discourages him from running much.

However, with his long legs, he can stride and keep pace with her.

"They met at a Bible academy in Frankfort, Ind., where he enrolled at age 14. He went there on his own initiative and worked his way through high school and college.

"At 2PM, on the day of a crusade, Clyde Dupin disappears. He retreats into his hotel room for four hours. He takes no calls, talks to no one. He insists on this.

For four straight hours, he is by himself, to read, study meditate and pray. He sorts through fact- filled notebooks. He reads articles from some 35 or 40 news magazines and religious periodicals to which he subscribes. He occasionally listens to tapes of earlier sermons to see 'if I might improve on something or see where I left something hanging.'

"He preaches a message of hope, forgiveness, and life changing possibilities. He uses no notes, and almost each one of his sentences in a long, 35-minute sermon is complete. Wes believes his father has a photographic memory. One night he counted 38 different scripture quotes in one of his father's messages.

"Dupin gets himself prepared to preach 'a simple salvation message that transcends denominational lines.' He's not interested in promoting one denomination or tearing down another -- that would be disastrous for an evangelist. 'I preach Christ and Christ crucified. There are not too many people who would not be in agreement on that.'

"By early evening, when he meets with the executive committee to go over details of the service, he is ready to go. His Bible is in hand.

In contrast to most crusades, attendance has gone up steadily. Usually the first night draws a large, curious crowd, then it falls off sharply and builds up to a grand finale the eighth night.

"In Corydon the crowds grow steadily: 1,288 for the opening service; 1,450 on Monday night; 1,600 the next night. The number of decisions has also increased for the first three nights. The Rev. Lyle Rasmussen, a United Methodist minister and an old friend and admirer of Clyde Dupin, who invited the evangelist to bring his team to Harrison County, says, before the Wednesday night crusade, 'Many decisions have already been made -- and that's what the crusade is all about.'"

The foregoing report, written by Randy West for the *CORYDON DEMOCRAT,* is a published representative of many such stories about the Clyde Dupin Crusades published in scores of local newspapers where crusades have been held. Because of the evangelist's integrity, his above board policies regarding finances and his insistence of local committees handling all the money, he has never been questioned about the budgetary aspects of a crusade. Each area crusade is responsible for developing its own budget and attempts to raise a large part before the actual crusade. When the local budget has been met, if there is a surplus, it goes to the work of the Clyde Dupin ministry. His salary does not come from this fund; it is determined and paid by his board of directors.

"Our only business is soul-winning and crusades," he says. His organization stages at least one missionary crusade each year outside the United States and the Clyde Dupin Ministries pays for that. One such crusade recently in Haiti, which cost about $19,000 was financed entirely by his organization.

Small-town newspapers across America headline the events of the Clyde Dupin Crusades. In the mountain town of Kingwood, West Virginia, population 2,550, the Book of Acts came alive November, 1979, as Dupin preached night after night to 1,500 who packed the new Civic Center. Some nights there were sleet and snow, but the people came anyway, filling the auditorium. As one person stated, "Clyde Dupin preaches them back."

Probably one of the secrets of Clyde's drawing power is his positive, dynamic presentation of his message. He speaks as one having authority. He would be the first to tell you he gets his authority from God's Word. As Dr. George Failing said, "There's always a ring of freshness in Clyde Dupin's preaching. Each sermon seems to be particularly prepared for that occasion."

Dupin kept his promise he had made earlier at a leadership banquet in Kingwood, when he said, "The Bible will be my text-book. I will emphasize the things Christ died for--Christ is the answer. In a world which has lost its way, people are ready to listen to a man who says he knows the way out."

People did listen in Kingwood. One night an entire football team was saved. Over 440 persons came forward and accepted Christ. "This crusade is the greatest thing that has ever happened in this county," stated Harry Mikels, Pastor of the United Methodist Church of Kingwood. "And I feel certain there is no other man in America that could bring the message and unite the people of our area like Clyde Dupin."

Similar things are said wherever Clyde Dupin and his team go. In Rutherfordton, North Carolina, the stadium was packed nightly with a total attendance of 20,000 and 500 decisions were made for Christ.

Whether it be in Kingwood, West Virginia; Rutherfordton, North Carolina; Sussex County, New Jersey; Shelbyville, Indiana; Wilkes-Barre, Pennsylvania; overseas in St. Croix, Virgin Islands; Barbados, West Indies; wherever the locale or whatever the type of audience, the message and the approach is the same because men's needs are the same regardless of location.

"'All have sinned and come short of the glory of God,' but Jesus Christ can forgive your sins. You can leave here tonight a changed person. You can be born again," Dupin tells his listeners in a strong forceful voice.

Sunday, June 8, 1980, the opening day for the Clyde Dupin Crusade in Asheboro, North Carolina, dawned bright and clear. By 5:30 P. M., 300 teenagers had gathered downtown to march the two miles to the football stadium for the opening night of the Dupin Crusade. At 7:30 P. M., the 2,300 seat stadium was full and 300 choir members filled the bleachers on the field in front of the stadium. John Innes was at the organ and Wes Dupin was urging the audience to do what the song they were about to sing said to do-- "Stand Up For Jesus."

Clyde Dupin's first sermon at the Asheboro Crusade set the pattern for all those to follow during the next week. He took his text from Mark 16:15, 16. "And he said unto them, go ye into all the world and preach the gospel to every creature. He that believeth and is baptized shall be saved; but he that believeth not shall be damned." All week long Dupin insisted that everyone must be born again. Hundreds heeded Dupin's message and were born again.

There were special guests to enhance the program by giving their testimonies in word or song. Lt. Clebe McClary, a Viet Nam hero, brought the audiences to their feet in a standing ovation as he shared how God brought him home after he almost lost his life in a fierce battle where many of his men died. Suzanne Johnson, a former Miss Illinois and Miss America runner-up, thrilled the audience with her beautiful soprano voice as she sang "The King Is Coming."

The news media gave excellent coverage the entire week of the crusade. The Greensboro Daily News, 26 miles away, devoted more than one full page to the Dupin Crusade, stating it was the most outstanding event in the history of

Asheboro. Never had any event in Asheboro made such an impact on their community. Over 4,000 had filled the stadium and spilled over on to the ground the last night of the crusade.

Ken Dupin

One crusade the Dupin Team will never forget was back in March, 1978. The day dawned bright and cool. It certainly did not seem like the kind of day that would turn into a crisis. It was during the Clyde Dupin Crusade in Altavista, Virginia that the day turned to near tragedy. All week long the gymnasium had been packed. Ken, the younger son of Clyde and Grace, had come to sing as special guest on Friday, "Youth Night." It was a great evening, Ken sang beautifully.

At 7:00 A.M. the next morning, Ken knocked lightly on Wes' motel door. The two boys had agreed to appear on a local radio talk show that morning. "What's the matter, Ken?" Wes asked. "You don't look very well."

"I don't feel too well," he replied, "but I promised I would go with you to the radio station, so let's go."

At 8:30 that morning the phone rang in the Dupins' motel room. Grace answered. "Hello," she said.

"Mom, something has happened to Ken," Wesley said in an alarmed voice on the other end of the line.

"What's wrong?" she demanded. "Mom, Ken has had a heart attack."

"I can't believe it! I can't believe it!" she cried. "He was fine last night."

Well, it was hard to believe that this fun loving, healthy appearing 23 year old young man could be struck down by a heart attack. Just the night before he had sung with such radiance and joy. But it was true.   Ken   was   rushed   by ambulance to a Lynchburg, Virginia, hospital. Ken was in critical condition. The cardiologist gave the family a very grave report. He said there was no help for him at the Lynchburg Hospital. He would have to be moved to Duke University Hospital where they might be able to help Ken with surgery.

The Dupins' family physician, Dr. Wesley Phillips, flew in from Kernersville to visit Ken and encourage the family. He also confirmed what the cardiologist had said, "Ken should be moved to Duke for surgery."

Ken was sent to Duke University Hospital where extensive tests were run. It was determined there that Ken had was known as Wolfe-Parkinson-White Syndrome, or simply, "a heart that runs away."

During these difficult times at Duke, not knowing from one day to the next if he would live, Ken and his wife, Joy, were greatly encouraged and comforted by a visit from Dr. and Mrs. Leighton Ford, friends of the Dupins. Ford related to Ken that his son, Sandy, had a similar heart problem, and Sandy had been in the same ward where Ken was at Duke Hospital.

A few weeks later, Ken underwent open heart surgery at Duke. It has been a long, hard road of recovery; but Ken returned to college and planned for a career in the ministry.

Protestant
Phenomenon
in Haiti

13

Protestant
Phenomenon in Haiti

For the past few years, the Clyde Dupin team has conducted at least one missionary crusade each year in a foreign land. Successful crusades were held in St. Croix and Barbados during 1977 and 1978.

An inquiry was received at the Kernersville headquarters from Dr. Claude Noel, the executive secretary of the Evangelical Council of Churches in Haiti in 1978, regarding the possibilities of a Clyde Dupin Crusade in Haiti, only 90-minutes by jet from Miami. Within a few days, the entire team was praying excitedly about the invitation but didn't realize that God was about to provide one of the biggest miracles in the history of the Clyde Dupin ministries.

Haiti, which means, "mountain land," is the second oldest republic in the Western hemisphere, with a population in excess of seven million, the majority living in spiritual and economic poverty. Seventy percent of the children are malnourished and 80 percent cannot read. Per capita income is only $125 per year.

The people are predominately Catholic, but voodoism and spiritualism is rampant among the superficial religious people.

A Haitian Phenomenon

"I believe God is going to do something great in Haiti" Clyde told his staff after the Lord had assured him that they must go to Port au Prince for a crusade. "But, I also believe that Satan will do everything in his power to thwart our efforts. We must earnestly pray for God's intervening," he added.

Thousands of supporters on the Dupin's mailing list were encouraged to pray daily for this expected great crusade. Hoover Smith, the overseas crusade director for the team, made many trips to Haiti to meet with Dr. Noel. Wes Dupin also went to speak in pre-crusade meetings with the local pastors and committees. Clyde and Grace continued in heavy-burdened prayer for the crusade each night, and claimed Ephesians 3:20 as an answer to their prayers: "Now unto him that is able to do exceeding abundantly above all that we ask or think, according to the power that worketh in us."

A miracle was needed. The rental of the 25,000 seat soccer stadium was staggering, as well as thousands of pieces of printed materials and Gospels of John, travel money for team members and all the incidental expenses incurred in such a crusade. The Dupins knew the poor Haitians could not help. They decided that no offerings could be taken during the crusade. The budget of $14,000 must be raised from their stateside supporters before they left home.

Only ten days before departure for Haiti, Eastern Airlines, who made all the travel arrangements for the team, phoned to report that all U.S. team members would have to produce a valid passport to enter the country. The Haitian Parliament had recently passed a new law to this effect and through much prayer and the help of the U.S. State Department in Washington, the team got a waiver from the new law until June 1.

On Sunday morning, March 4, the Clyde Dupin team spread across the city of Port an Prince in speaking engagements at churches to invite the people to the crusade meetings. They prayed that God would send at least 10,000 persons to the opening meeting on Sunday night. That afternoon, they planned a march through the streets of Port au Prince to interest the people in the crusade. More than 5,000 joined the march through the streets, led by a band playing, "Onward Christian Soldiers." Team members and volunteers passed out literature to the throngs who watched the parade.

At 6:30 PM Sunday evening, Ken Dupin rushed back to his father's hotel room to tell him, "Dad, the entire stadium is filled already. Thousands are standing on the field," he said excitedly. "They have already locked the gates and many thousands have been turned away."

As Clyde made his way to the stadium, he encountered some difficulty getting into the crusade. The throngs were still crowded around the entrance gates and it was difficult to find the doors. Not able to speak French or Creole, the language of the Haitians, he tried to find someone who could help him get into the stadium. He tried to explain that he was the evangelist and it was necessary for him to get in.

All his pleading was in vain. Finally, a stranger took him by the hand, apparently knowing that he was the honored speaker, and pushed through the crowd. The stranger found the gate, crawled under a locked turnstile and led Clyde to the podium.

A dark cloud in the West threatened a downpour as Clyde looked out on the sea of black faces, apparently hungry for the Gospel. His spirit was moved as he faced the largest crowd he had ever spoken to in his life. The urgency of the

Holy Spirit supported him as he went to the podium, following a tremendous preliminary song service.

It was harvest time in Haiti, where only 12 percent profess a personal faith in Christ. This week long crusade ushered in a new day for evangelicals. This was their first interdenominational crusade and the largest crowd ever assembled. When the last inquirer had been counseled, more than 17,000 persons had responded to the invitation and 200,000 had attended the crusade.

All attendance records for Haiti and the Clyde Dupin team had been broken. For the final service March 11, more than 10,000 people were in the stadium three hours before starting time. The stadium was completely packed with many thousands crowded close together on the field. When the gates were closed long before the final service started, 45,000 people were inside and thousands more were turned away.

Saturation Evangelism

The Haitian crusade was a program of saturation evangelism. There were twenty pastors and lay persons from the United States who joined the regular team to assist with the program of evangelism, speaking in many churches, schools, and the University. Grace Dupin conducted five Ladies Prayer Teas with total attendance of 3,000. Each week day there was street evangelism directed by Rev. Clarence Williams where more than 100,000 pieces of Gospel literature were distributed.

Dr. Wesley Phillips assisted in a hospital ministry and counseling. Concurrent with the crusade, a Pastor's School drew an average attendance of 225 ministers each day. Dr. George Failing directed the school while Dr. Bob Harrison, Dr. Clyde Parker and Rev. Allan Davis conducted the seminars and workshops. The Haitian pastors were taught methods of church growth, follow-up, discipleship and personal soul winning.

Radio Coverage

Each evening, crusade music and program director, Wes Dupin, led the great crowds in familiar Gospel songs. Wes and Ken Dupin, were also crusade vocalists. Bob Harrison, "America's Black Son of Thunder," was also guest soloist. Several nights, Haitian groups provided special music.

All eight services were broadcast to the entire country through a special radio network of relay stations by Radio Lumiere. The O.M.S. station in Cape Haitian beamed the program into Santo Domingo and Cuba. Since all other stations leave the air at 7 p.m., it was estimated that 2 million Haitians listened by radio each night. Many villages set up loud speakers to broadcast the services by radio.

The secular press gave excellent coverage to the crusade. In the last service, the Secretary of State and the President of Parliament were seated on the platform. Secretary of State, Gilot, urged Rev. Dupin to return again to Haiti.

One veteran missionary of 30 years in Haiti said, "This crusade has been like an oasis in the dessert."

Repeat Crusade

The Clyde Dupin team returned to El Sylvio Cator Soccer Stadium in Port au Prince, Haiti, again in 1980, to experience a repeat of God's special anointing. An additional 12,000 persons made personal decisions for Christ during the second crusade, with the stadium completely packed the last night. God's presence was evident during the entire second crusade, but one specific incident stands out vividly in Grace's mind.

The following story written by Grace Dupin was published in a Christian magazine soon after the crusade in Haiti. This story reveals the miracle working power of God even in the midst of spiritual darkness.

'Thanks, Old Man'

"I was seated in a metal folding chair on the grass in front of the high steel platform that had been erected in the center of the Sylvio Cator Stadium. The sun had already dipped over the bay and darkness had settled down on the beautiful but poor city of Port au Prince, Haiti. It was Sunday, March 10, 1980. I had accompanied my husband, Clyde Dupin, along with other members of our team for an eight-day evangelistic crusade in Port au Prince.

"All week long Clyde had preached his gospel messages with simplicity and power through a Haitian interpreter, Dr. Claude Noel. When the invitation was given each evening, all you could hear was the tramp, tramp, trampling of feet as hundreds came forward. Tonight was the last night of a wonderful week of crusade services. The excitement electrified the air as 45,000 people jammed into the stadium for this final service.

"The service was well underway. I was singing the songs of praise with the great congregation. My English words were mixed, mingled and drowned out by the Haitians' Creole as our songs of praise filled the dark, Caribbean sky.

"All of a sudden, my song froze in my throat as my eyes caught a glimpse of Clyde's face. It was drawn and deathly white. All evening I had been casting anxious glances toward the high platform where my husband was seated, because most of that day he had not felt well. Clyde dismissed it as nothing serious and came to the service prepared to preach. But his white, drawn face told me what I feared most; he was very ill, too ill to preach.

"Oh, God, I cried, how can such a terrible thing happen? Look at these thousands of people that have come to hear the message.' I knew there were other capable ministers on the platform who could fill in on a moments notice. But I also knew that this audience had grown to love Clyde Dupin and to switch speakers at the last moment would cause confusion and disappointment.

"I glanced fearfully back at Clyde. A team member, Steve Wingfield, was helping him off the platform down the high, wobbly steps. I thought he would faint and fall in a heap at the foot of the steps; but others came to the rescue and placed him in a chair behind the platform. Then he was overcome by vomiting. A nurse rushed to his side, but there was little she could do.

"I felt helpless and heartsick as I saw them preparing to put Clyde in a van and take him away.

"Then, out of the audience came an old, white haired Haitian man making his feeble way toward Clyde. He placed his weathered, brown hands on Clyde's bowed head and began to pray.

"I don't know what he said. I was not close enough to hear. But there was a glow that lit up the old man's face as he prayed. (Clyde told me later a warm, peaceful feeling swept over his body as the old man prayed).

"A miracle happened!

"I saw Clyde lift his head, sit up straight and wipe his face. He stood tall and erect, then walked back up those steep steps to the platform. Moments later he stepped to the microphone and preached a powerful message, 'Heaven Or Hell.' Thousands decided for heaven that night.

"Then the old man disappeared back into the night. Nobody thought to thank him for his prayer. But surely there will be thousands in heaven who will search him out of the crowd and thank him.

"The big Pan Am airplane taxied down the runway. Soon, Clyde Dupin was looking down on the little grass huts that dotted the countryside, overshadowed by the towering mountains of Haiti. The crusade was over. He was on his way back home to the United States.

"His country was rich in every aspect compared to Haiti. But God is not impressed by our riches or by our poverty. He pours his blessings on those who humble themselves and pray. 'If my people which are called by my name shall humble themselves and pray, and seek my face, and turn from their wicked ways, then will I hear from heaven and will forgive their sin and will heal their land.' (II Chronicles 7:14)

No matter whether Clyde Dupin is preaching at home or abroad to large crowds or small ones, the thing that impresses his close associates and friends is the life he lives behind the scenes. His humility is genuine. His walk with God is sincere. He lives what he preaches. Really. it can be said, 'He was born to be the evangelist.'"

14

This is Your Life

Over the years some things have never changed. Dupin still has that same common touch, same love for people and that same strong Southern accent. After a news conference in preparation for the Clyde Dupin Roanoke, Va., Crusade, in the fall of 1982, Frances Stebbins, of the Roanoke Times, wrote,

"Like Ronald Reagan, Clyde Dupin has a good stage presence, a direct way of speaking and a down-to-earth approach to what he sees as worries of the day. If the president thinks most problems will be solved by tinkering with the economy, Dupin sees them as being solved by turning one's life over to Jesus.

"Before a news conference, Dupin raises his voice and without notes delivers a 10 minute basic message of the world's need for Christ. He is positive and authoritative and effective," she concludes.

Whether he is preaching to 45,000 people in a packed soccer stadium in Port au Prince, Haiti, or crusades at home in high school stadiums and gyms, a conference in Jerusalem or to delegates at the International Conference for Evangelists in Amsterdam, Holland, his message is always preached with simplicity, clarity, intensity, and compassion ... the results have been tremendous.

As many as 20,000 people, in a single year, make decisions for Christ in his crusades. In the summer of 1982, Dupin visited Russia and Poland as a member of "The International Study League."

There he saw first-hand the oppression of a communistic government upon the Church. There were only 21 functioning churches in Leningrad, Russia, for the 5,000,000 people. There were no Sunday Schools in Russia. Christians could not advance in their careers; and many of the true believers had to worship underground.

The citizens of Poland had more freedom of worship than the Russian people; but they were still under the iron fist of a communistic government that oppressed them every day of their lives. One Polish man confided to Dupin, "The Polish people will never give up. We will continue to fight for our freedom."

But Clyde knows that real oppression comes from Satan. No lasting freedom or peace can be found until a person accepts Christ. This is why Dupin has spent most of his life preaching the Gospel.

To Honor a Life
The Clyde Dupin Ministries' Board of Directors wanted to honor such a life. They chose Dupin's 50th birthday, in 1983, to celebrate his 20 years in full-time evangelism.

"This is your life, Clyde Dupin!" boomed from the loud speakers, as a surprised Clyde, along with Grace, entered the banquet room. Some 350 friends from 15 states had gathered, on a Friday evening, at the Holiday Inn in Greensboro, North Carolina, for an honor banquet and a "This Is Your Life" program.

Among the participants were family members, crusade converts, a most recent one, Delano Wood of the famous Wood Brothers racing family: Bruce Meads, the imprisoned soldier who had written letters of encouragement from Germany, to Clyde when he was a young Christian: Ola Langley, the dear woman, who had sent money when they had no money: Clarence Williams, the converted alcoholic, who is now an outstanding pastor.

There were close friends, including guest soloists, Suzanne Johnson and Bob Harrison. Bill Glass spoke warmly of his close relationship with Dupin through many years of evangelism.

The feeling of the board members was probably expressed best by Russ Roberts, who has been chairman of the board since 1980. He and his wife Helen have traveled with the Dupins many times to Haiti, Africa, and the Middle East.

He says, "Most people are trying to find someone to believe in, someone they can trust; yet they are afraid, for fear that when they get to know the real person they will be disappointed. But I have known Clyde intimately for many years; He's one man I've never been disappointed in. His integrity, uprightness, honesty and commitment are unquestionable."

The exciting evening was climaxed when Dr. John Newby, president of Central Wesleyan College, conferred upon Dupin, the Doctor of Divinity degree.

In his presentation President Newby said, "Central Wesleyan College honors Clyde Dupin for lovingly, tenderly and faithfully preaching the Gospel of Jesus Christ throughout the world."

This memorable evening was exciting and a blessing to all who attended. It was an evening that highlighted 20 years of success in evangelism.

But no one is more surprised by the success of his ministry than Clyde himself. Someone asked Grace, "What's his real secret of success?"

"It's a combination of things," Grace smiled. "He is persistent and works hard. He has a deep spiritual commitment to his work. He lives, breaths and sleeps the Gospel; but most of all he has a disciplined prayer life."

And Clyde would be quick to tell you an evangelist's life is not always easy. It means constant travel, living out of a suitcase, getting used to new beds every week or so, and eating in restaurants. It means dealing with emotional pressures-- financial struggles of a faith ministry, the strain of preparing a sermon night after night trying to make some of the same old messages sound new and exciting.

"I'm just an ordinary preacher with an extra ordinary mission," he declares. "But I've known from boyhood days that my major mission in life is to do the work of an evangelist."

Majors on Essentials

Certainly Clyde has a God-given gift of preaching which he has developed and exercised. Because of this, thousands each year come to know Christ as their personal Savior. He seems to belong to all churches and to Christians everywhere, not because he has compromised but because he majors on the great essentials of the Christian Faith. Because of Dupin's great love for the church, he is often referred to as "an evangelist with a pastor's heart."

He feels his mission is to help bring renewal to the local churches and to assist the pastors in reaping a harvest of lost souls. Each year Clyde has many speaking engagements. But his most important work is the citywide crusades.

During 1983 his crusade schedule included: Goanives, Haiti; Ft. Scott, Kansas; Stuart, Virginia; Ashland, Kentucky; Martinsburg, Pennsylvania; Excelsior Springs, Missouri; Bedford, Virginia; and Washington Court House, Ohio.

After he returned to Washington Court House, Ohio, for a second crusade, a local pastor, Dr. Stan Toler stated, "I have been privileged to work in two city-wide crusades with Clyde Dupin. I know of no one who does a better job in crusade evangelism. When he leaves town finances will be in order, goals for the crusade will be reached and most of all, souls will be won!"

Eden, North Carolina

Reporter Chuck Alston of the *Greensboro Daily News*, describes a typical Clyde Dupin Crusade service in Eden, North Carolina;

"Monday night at 7:15, the stadium was full. On the field, the choir had squeezed in its last bit of practice. The evangelist, Clyde Dupin, and his crusade team were going over the evening's sequence.

"The evangelist downplayed his role. 'I sometimes tell people I'm like the Western Union boy: I just deliver the message,' Dupin said.

"They prayed.

"Nearby, the Rev. Barry Smith, pastor of First Baptist Church and chief local counselor for the crusade, was hustling toward another last-minute detail. 'I'm about worn out.' Smith allowed between huffs. 'But this is tremendous. I love it! I love it! This is the greatest thing that ever happened.'

"At 7:27, Wes Dupin, the evangelist's son, opened the crusade with the enthusiasm that would characterize the next 90 minutes. A booming 'Blessed Assurance' beckoned the approaching night. Along the way it gathered momentum with celebration and prayer, song and testimony of the power of God and his Son, Jesus Christ. But the evening would hinge on the Evangelist's message of salvation.

"And the man can preach.

"Dupin, wired with a cordless Sony microphone, captured the crowd at 8:15 with informal chat, and didn't turn it loose until it was almost nine o'clock and dark. The message, as promised, was simple: by being born again, a person can be at peace in both life and death.

"I believe that the greatest need in our society is that men and women would come to know the Lord Jesus Christ.

"The Bible tells a similar story of a powerful man coming to understand 'born again.'" And Dupin, a Bible preacher, would draw repeatedly on the book of John, in which Jesus meets Nicodemus on a moonlit street corner of Old Jerusalem and tells the powerful Pharisee:

"'Verily, verily, I say unto thee, except a man be born again, he cannot see the kingdom of God... except a man be born of water and of the Spirit, he cannot enter into the Kingdom of God. That which is born of the flesh is flesh and that which is born of the spirit is spirit.'

"You tonight in this service can become a born again Christian,' Dupin said. 'You have no promise of tomorrow. Tonight is your night of opportunity.'

"With those words, Dupin bade the crowd to come forward. Forty responded. An old man shook his hand. A tearful family huddled around its mother. A teenager, arms folded over the fence, wept openly.

"Still he continued, his 6'4" frame swaying, powerful arms swinging, his face glistening from the sweat of 40 minutes of non-stop preaching: "Tonight can be your night of nights. Your life can be changed, your sins forgiven. God loves you. Christ died for your sins. Don't wait until it's too late. Don't wait until tomorrow ... it may never come for some of us here. Come to Christ and he'll give You peace.

"As the choir sang the invitation, many came forward. Night two of the eight-day crusade was over. Night three was less than 24 hours away.

"After the crusade is over Dupin goes home to Kernersville, a small town in the Piedmont area of North Carolina. Much of his time at home is spent in his Kernersville office directing the activities of the Clyde Dupin Ministries, Inc."

The Dupin Family: Clyde and Grace, l-r, Scott and Joy George, Wes, Claudia, Joy, Ken

An invitation to accept Christ at Battle Creek, MI Crusade, 1984

*Clyde Dupin
speaking at
Gonaives,Haiti
Crusade, 1983*

*Over 7,000
attend the
Roanoke, Virginia
Crusade, 1982*

President Newby, Central Wesleyan College, confers Doctor of Divinity Degree on Clyde. Dr. Clyde Parker on right.

Clyde with Crusade Chairmen in tribal dress, Nigeria, West Africa

Clyde, Grace and Bob Harrison at Amsterdam International Conference for Evangelists.

Clyde Dupin and Charles Stanley share a laugh.

Clyde Dupin with Music Director Rick Webb.

C. R. and Jo Byrd, Grace, Clyde, Barbara and Dudley Simms.

Board Chairman, Russ Roberts, presents a $10,000 check to Clyde for office project.

Clyde visits Leningrad, Russia, 1982.

Grace and Clyde visit Jerusalem.

Former Kentucky Governor Julian Carroll with Dr. Dupin.

Dr. Clyde Dupin with South Dakota Governor Miller.

*Dr. Dupin Preached to a full house at the
Drama Theater in Vladimi, Russia, in 1993.*

*It was standing room only for the Dupin
Crusade in Murom, Russia, in 1995.*

(left) The Mayor of Tula, Russia, welcomes Dr. Dupin to his city for a Crusade

(Right) Mayor of Murom, Russia, accepts a Bible from Dr. Dupin.

(Above) In Red Square, Moscow, Dr. Dupin met with Dr. Bill Bright of Campus Crusade, and North Carolina businessman Dudley Simms.

(Right) Vladimir, Russia, Mayor Igor Shamov, who attended the nightly crusades, welcomed Dr.Dupin to his city.

The Dupins are welcome to Sanski Most, Bosnia,
by Mayor Alagica and his wife.

Dr. Dupin preached to an all Muslim crowd
in Sanski Most, Bosnia.

*Dr. Dupin placed flowers at a mass grave
near Sanski Most, Bosnia.*

*Dr. Dupin stands with UN escort Major Seawood in Mostar,
Bosinia, where a preaching service was held.*

*Clyde Dupin extends invitation to accept Christ
at a crusade in Zagreb, Croatia, in 1998.*

*Dr. Dupin with Col. Khure, Deputy Commander
of UN Forces in Bosnia.*

Grace and Clyde Dupin, 1998

Clyde Dupin Board members (1998)
(Standing) Fred Murrow, Paul Taylor, James Shelor, Ed Johnson, Leroy
Vernon, Charlie Schram, Jack Greenwood, Bob Hine, and Everrett Conrad.
(Seated) Jerry Snyder, Ben Davis, Elaine Mohl, Grace Dupin, Clyde Dupin,
Larry Butts. Wesley Philips, Dale Hileman, and Dick Gerber.

15

A Global Outreach

Clyde said he felt a great surge of joy as he looked down on Amsterdam, Holland, from the plane window of KLM's 747, as it approached the International Airport. Amsterdam is a beautiful, world famous, city with flowing canals, lined with red roofed townhouses.

Amsterdam

Dupin had been invited by Dr. Billy Graham to speak at the International Conference for Itinerant Evangelists in Amsterdam. The time had arrived and he felt honored to be part of this great worldwide conference.

On the hot, humid evening of Saturday 12, July 1983 the International Conference of Itinerant Evangelists, Amsterdam '83, opened in the great hall of the RAI. As John Innes played the organ, a citizen of every country, which was represented, brought his national flag to the platform in a wave of colorful procession. Flag after flag came by until 132 flags flowed in the soft summer breeze that evening.

After the ceremonies of welcome, Billy Graham brought a stirring message entitled, "The Evangelist in a Torn World."

Dupin was one of five ministers who was asked to speak on "How To Give An Invitation For People To Commit Their Lives To Jesus Christ." Clyde's message to the evangelists was "Glorify God in all that you do. In giving an invitation, be aware that it is 'Not by might nor by power, but by my spirit, saith the Lord.' (Zechariah 4:6)

"The successful invitation must be bathed in prayer. Only men of prayer can give an invitation with love, compassion and genuine concern for lost souls. Men of prayer know the public invitation must never be a gimmick to trick people; but it is an urgent invitation to accept Jesus Christ.

"The method of giving an invitation," Dupin said, "is not nearly as important as the commitment, integrity and Spirit filled life of the messenger who gives that invitation. The cross must always be central in your preaching. And the Holy Spirit must be the power behind your message."

Meeting Friends

Not only was Dupin's message a blessing to his fellow evangelists but it was a joyous conference for Clyde and Grace where they met old friends from other countries where Dupin had conducted crusades. They met new, third world friends, who had never traveled outside of their own country. And it was a joy to meet and fellowship with well known ministers from around the world.

Dr. Gordon Moyes, pastor of Wesley Central Mission, a multi-faceted Christian center of Sydney Australia, became a delightful friend. It was also a thrill to meet and fellowship with

Dr. Paul Cho, pastor of the largest church in the world in Seoul, Korea.

The conference ended after 10 days with a great service of Holy Communion conducted by the Bishop of Norwich from England, and with a challenge from Dr. Graham in his final address,... "that while the social needs of man call for our urgent attention, we believe that ultimately these needs can be met only in and through the Gospel. Man's basic need is to be converted to Christ. Man must be changed. Man's biggest problem is man himself."

It was a great conference of spiritual renewal which only the future can measure. The message is always the same. This same message of Jesus Christ has been interpreted into many different languages: and it always works when it is preached in the power of the Holy Spirit.

An Unchanging Message

Clyde feels that God has called him to preach this message ... primarily in crusade evangelism. Nothing is going to deter him from this ministry. He has visited 35 countries and has shared God's word with over 2,000,000 people face to face. He wants to preach the gospel to as many people as possible, as long as he lives.

If there is one thing that has been a staying power in Dupin's expanding ministry it is his determination to keep Christ the central theme of his message and to keep his deep love for people. Whether he is talking with one person or speaking to large audiences, he has instant rapport. Each individual feels loved.

The editor of a Bluffton, Indiana, newspaper, Jim Barbieri, said "When you interview Clyde Dupin some overwhelming facts shine through. He is a realist with a decisive outlook, he loves Jesus Christ and he loves people."

It was because of this love and desire to win souls that Dupin and his team went to Africa. In the summer of 1984 the team boarded a Nigerian jumbo jet in New York city to wing their way across the vast Atlantic Ocean to Lagos, Nigeria, in West Africa. It was to have been a non-stop flight to Lagos, but the plane was so overloaded with passengers in every seat and way too much baggage in the cargo bay, that the plane had to make an unscheduled stop in Dakar, Senegal. When the plane touched down on the runway a tire was damaged. A replacement had to be flown in from another country which took several hours. What was to have been a 12 hour non-stop flight from New York to Lagos turned into a long and weary 18 hour trip.

Of course, by the time Dupin and his team reached Lagos they had missed their flight to Calabar where a group of African Christians were waiting at the airport to give them a grand welcome and take them on to Uyo. The disappointed group had to return the 50 miles back to Uyo; but they were all back the next day with happy, smiling faces to welcome Dupin and his team.

Clyde Dupin has learned that world situations are so changeable that he must walk through doors when they open. For over two decades there has been a constant changing of governments, boundaries, and leaders in Africa. Almost every nation in Africa has been battered by internal fighting and revolution. Many of the missionaries have been forced to leave the continent. But the vast majority of the African people hunger after the gospel.

One dear African woman came to Mrs. Dupin when the crusade was almost over and said, "Please, will your team come back to our country. Our 'stomachs' so hunger after God!"

This hunger was evident as Clyde preached for eight nights in the soccer stadium. This soccer field was also a graveyard. Hundreds had been buried in this soccer field some years before when there had been a civil war. The people did not let the fact that their relatives were buried in this very place, where we were having the crusade services, keep them from attending. Night after night the people came and stood for the entire service in rapt attention. When the invitation was given each evening, men, women, children, and sometime entire families would rush to the front to accept Christ.

After Dupin returned home from the African crusade he was convinced anew that human nature is the same the world over -- man hungers after God. When the Gospel is preached in simplicity and power the human soul will respond.

Today Dupin has unbounded opportunities to minister throughout the world. He has invitations to conduct crusades in many African countries, India, Philippine Islands, Australia, and several Caribbean countries.

"You're never the same after you have been to Haiti, Africa, South America and the mission fields of our world," Dupin says. "I have looked into the pleading eyes of these people, and sensed the loneliness and pain in their lives. I have seen thousands respond to the Gospel; and I could almost see the light of Jesus dispel the darkness."

Haiti captured the heart of Dupin the first time he visited there. The one overriding thought that seized him, as he looked down on Port au Prince from the big Pan Am airplane, after the 1980 crusade, was "I must return with the Gospel. There are thousands who are steeped in superstitions, voodoo worship and multitudes who have never once heard the message of Jesus Christ.

Return to Haiti
"After I visited Haiti and saw the poverty, material things mean very little to me. The world is passing away; what

I do for Christ I must do quickly. I don't have a desire for money except as I might use it to help spread the gospel," Clyde said.

So it has been with great compassion that Dupin has returned with his team, year after year to the poor country of Haiti with the saving message of Jesus Christ. The results have been tremendous. Not only have thousands attended the nightly crusades services, but Dupin's messages have been broadcast throughout the entire country by radio. As a result of his broad ministry and love for the Haitian people, he has become a well known and greatly respected figure among the pastors and people of Haiti.

In 1981 Dupin returned to the beautiful seaport town of Cape Haitian for a six day crusade. In 1982 he went to Les Cayes.

Goanives, Haiti was the city of the 1983 crusade. This endeavor was blessed with a great spirit of co-operation among the local pastors. The 500 voice choir, made up of young people from the area churches, was superb. There was a floodtide of goodwill and spiritual hunger.

Bob Hines, one of Dupin's board members, who has assisted in many of the overseas campaigns said, "The Goanives crusade was one of the most thrilling ones I have participated in. God's presence was there nightly, in a powerful way."

The services were held in the city park, located in the center of Goanives. About a half block from the crusade site was a prison. Each evening the prisoners would climb up into the barred windows and listen to the beautiful singing of the congregation and to the simple but powerful message of Dupin. As the service blared out over the P.A. system, God did his work in that prison. In the most miserable conditions imaginable, many of those prisoners gave their hearts to Christ.

The last Sunday afternoon of the crusade several of the

team members went into that miserable prison and ministered to those babes in Christ. Even the darkest of prison walls cannot keep God's light from shining through. "To open their eyes and to turn them from darkness to light, and from the power of Satan unto God," (Acts 26:18).

"I would preach a life time," Clyde says, "for the thrill of seeing just one person come to Christ, yet I have seen thousands."

The last week in February of 1985, Dupin and his team flew back to Port au Prince. There a big, tough, yellow landrover was rented from the Cribbean Christian Center. This was the only transportation that was suitable for the 130 miles of high, treacherous, mountain road that led into the seacoast city of Jeremie.

Larry Crotts, crusade director for the Jeremie crusade said, "What was accomplished in Jeremie the week of the crusade was a miracle of God. The last night 25,000 people heard Clyde call sinners to repentance and faith in Jesus Christ. There were 4,400 who made decisions for Christ. There was a total attendance of over 100,000 people. Many of these had to walk several miles each evening to attend."

Shipboard Salvation

God worked a miracle, for a ship load of people, on Friday night of the Jeremie crusade. Clyde and Grace were standing on the balcony of the Cabana Hotel waiting for the landrover to come and take them to the evening service. In the distance they could see a ship in the bay; it was in trouble. It was listing badly to one side. For two days this banana boat had been in the Jeremie Port loading its cargo. By the time it was ready to set sail to Port au Prince it was overloaded with grain, fresh produce, charcoal, live animals and about 800 passengers. These passengers were seated on top of all the cargo.

Just as the Dupins were arriving at the wharf, the crusade site, the stricken vessel was pulling alongside port just a few feet away from the platform where Dupin would preach that evening. All 800 passengers on board the ship could hear his message. As Clyde preached he offered those 18,000 on the wharf and those 800 on the ship a message of hope, new life in Christ and eternal salvation.

When Dupin gave the invitation that evening for sinners to receive Christ into their life he also turned to those on the stricken freighter and said, "I know you passengers on the ship cannot come forward; but if you would like to accept Christ into your heart, raise your hand."

Hands went up all over the ship. "Now, please pray the sinner's prayer of repentance with me and accept Jesus Christ into your heart." Many prayed aloud on the ship and were saved. What a miracle!

The Evangelical Council of Churches in Haiti under the direction of Dr. Claude Noel, had their first National Consultation on Evangelism during the Jeremie Crusade. The Christian leaders and pastors attended seminars and workshops during the day and came to the crusade at night. Dupin addressed the pastors and challenged them to get the Haitian churches involved in both personal and mass evangelism.

Dr. Noel said, "Clyde Dupin preaches the simple Gospel in a way that everyone understands. The tremendous response to his messages surprises many. Through the influence of his ministry several new churches have been built in Haiti, medical supplies, farm equipment, a tractor and large van have been sent for missionary work.

Each year his organization provides thousands of booklets and gospel literature for overseas evangelism. These Faith missionary projects are made possible by the gifts of friends who support his ministry. His major ministry, however, is to the cities and county seat towns of America. Perhaps, this is why the media often refer to him as "the Billy Graham of the small cities". Clyde Dupin, a servant of God, who was born to be the evangelist, will always be a man restless to win souls.

16

Open Doors to Russia

In the summer of 1982, Dr. Dupin visited Leningrad, the second largest city (since renamed St. Petersburg), in the Soviet Union, as a member of the International Study League.

"Our tour was under constant surveillance," Clyde said. "Armed guards stood outside our hotel door. We hardly had the privilege to talk with a Russian citizen."

For many years Communist leaders had tried to tell their people everything was fine; but the Russian people joke about themselves, "Adam and Eve were Russian, you know; they were improperly clothed, possessed only one apple between them, and someone was always telling them they lived in paradise!"

"It was evident there was no paradise here," Clyde relates. "I never forgot those pleading eyes of loneliness and pain a communistic government had brought to their lives. I prayed that someday I could return to tell these lost, deceived, unhappy people that Christ is alive and can save them from their sins and give them eternal life."

First Crusade in Russia

Ten years later the Iron Curtain came down, and many believed through a miracle of God. In April 1992, the door opened for Dr. Dupin and his team to go to Vladimir, Russia, a city one hundred miles east of Moscow, with a population of 360,000.

Hoover Smith, a good friend, who helped Dupin in other Crusades, had a great hand in opening this door because of a business project his son-in-law was working on in Vladimir.

A warm invitation was extended to Dupin by Mayor Igro Shamov, of Vladimir. He hosted a press conference for Dupin and invited government leaders and educators to attend.

Dr. Dupin reminded those present, "Many of the great cathedrals in Russia were closed for 70 years, but communism never closed the hunger for God in the hearts of her people. There is a new spirit of trust and friendship between our countries. But, faith in God gives us a moral standard to live by, also, for our families and our government, but greatest of all, it gives a relationship with God."

The Gospel had not been preached in Vladimir, openly, for more than 70 years. Alexander Solzhenitsyn, a Russian dissident in exile, said, "Over half a century ago, while I was still a child, I recall hearing a number of older people offer the following explanation for the great disasters that had befallen Russia: 'Men have forgotten God; that's why all this has happened.'"

Solzhenitsyn went on to say, "I myself see Christianity today as the only spiritual force capable of undertaking the spiritual healing of Russia ."

Vladimir still retains some of its beauty. Some of the most beautiful Russian Orthodox Cathedrals in the world adorn the hills surrounding the city. It seems a miracle that any would survive the purge and destruction by the Communist Government. Of course, many did not survive. Some of the churches were turned into KGB headquarters, some into art museums, others into storage facilities. There were only three small Protestant churches in the large city.

Grace, along, with other team members visited one of these surviving Orthodox Churches. A service was in progress. An audience of about 100 stood the entire time. There was such a hunger and pain etched on their faces. There was no joy, or peace and no salvation message.

First Service

The first Crusade service was held in the soccer stadium, it was cold and snowing; but the Gospel was welcomed with great joy and excitement.

The grandmothers, with their babushka, (scarf covered heads), young girls with ruddy cheeks and sparkling eyes, young men, old men, and children all came to the soccer stadium on that cold snowy Saturday afternoon, where Dr. Dupin preached his first Crusade message in Vladimir.

The first service was at 3:00 p.m. with another at 6:00 p.m. It was a never to be forgotten afternoon.

The next services were moved into the beautiful Drama Hall. Hundreds of people stood in line waiting for the doors to open. The auditorium was filled quickly, even into the balcony.

The eager audience that overflowed the Drama Hall each evening heard Dr. Dupin along, with his excellent translator, Oleg Shevkum, loaned by the Billy Graham office in Moscow, preach a God anointed message. Dupin and Oleg became so efficient preaching and translating together it could hardly be detected when one stopped and the other began.

Mayor Shamov attended the Sunday service. He told Clyde afterwards that he welcomed his ministry for having a positive impact on the city's people. "What you have brought to this city is most needed by our people. You've brought them faith and hope," Shamov said with a warm smile. From this time on Mayor Shamov became a great asset in helping the Clyde Dupin Crusades. He would call the mayor of the next city where Dupin was going telling him to help in every way possible.

Clyde shared with them the longing he found common to people everywhere. There is emptiness, loneliness, guilt and the fear of death. "Never in my life have I been among people with a more ravenous appetite for God", Dupin relates.

Rick and Phyllis Webb, with Bob Andersen as accompanist, would give an inspiring mini concert each evening before Dr. Dupin preached. Oh, how the Russian people loved to clap along as the Webbs sang many of the songs. "The Longer I serve Him the Sweeter He Grows," seemed to be one of the people's favorites.

After Dupin preached each evening he gave an invitation for people to accept Christ. At times, a large percent of the audience would respond. Service after service it was the same great numbers coming forward to receive Christ.

There were three older women, with scarf covered heads, who came to Grace after one such service. "We have ridden the train from Suzdal (A town some distance away), to hear your husband preach and to receive a Bible. By the time we pushed our way to the front all the Bibles were gone."

They started to weep. That was more than Grace could bear. Of course, she had no intention of turning them away empty handed. A Bible was found for each lady. They were thrilled to receive this most precious book; each put her arms around Grace and kissed her on both checks.

Other Services

In addition to the Crusade rallies, Dr. Dupin spoke in schools, colleges and prisons. Grace Dupin, spoke twice each day in schools, colleges and hospitals. A team of four businessmen, George McCrory of Best Locks, Dudley Simms, former owner of a chain of Piece Goods Shops, Ronnie Parker of CAP Care, and Bob Hill of Hillwood Ministries, shared the free enterprise system of U.S. businesses. They concluded their presentation with a witness of their personal faith in Christ and invited them to attend the Crusade.

When Dupin was speaking at the Science Research Center, where weapons of war were brought into reality, there was a large bust of Lenin behind him, as if watching in disapproval. "All I knew to do in this place, was to preach the Gospel," Dupin said. "When I gave a simple invitation for those present who would like to receive Jesus, I was overwhelmed when fifty of these highly trained scientists stood to receive Christ."

Victor Krukovsky, was one of these scientists, who was the former Secretary of the Communist Party and had a Ph.D. in Science. Earlier in the week of the Crusade Victor had asked Dr. Dupin to have lunch with him. It was during the course of this luncheon that Victor accepted Christ.

Svetlana

Another early convert was Svetlana, (we called her Lana), who was Dr. Dupin's charming, fluent in English, translator and guide. She met the Dupin Team at the airport in Moscow along with a bus and drivers who would stay with the group their entire mission in Russia. It was on this bus ride to

Vladimir, Lana leaned across the isle to speak with Clyde, "I know why you people have come to Russia. You are here for religious services," she said. " Please don't push religion on me." But Lana was soon won over.

In one of the first Crusades services as Lana listened to Dr. Dupin preach a simple salvation message, her heart was touched, she stood to receive Christ. What a thrill to see her hunger grow for Christ the following days. This beautiful highly educated woman has become a dear friend of the Dupins. What a blessing she has become in the Crusades to follow in other Russian cities.

Return to Russia

In early October 1992, Dr. Dupin returned to Russia. As his plane dipped below the cloud cover in its initial approach into Moscow airport he could again see the shabby construction of row after row of high-rise apartment buildings. Everything looked alike, shabby and run-down.

Parked on side, on unused runways were a great number of planes from the national airline, Aeroflot. Probably too old to fly and no money for repairs.

Once inside Moscow's International Airport you were made to wonder, "Why don't they turn the lights on?" But it was the same the last time, only a bulb here and there was burning. But Dr. Dupin was back to bring a message that burns away all darkness and share the Light that never burns out.

Back in Vladimir

After a three hour bus ride from Moscow the Clyde Dupin Team had returned to Vladimir for their second Crusade. The group included 24 professional people and pastors. Mayor Shamov was excited to see the Dupin Team return for a second Crusade. Again he hosted a press conference and encouraged the news media to give maximum coverage to all Dupin's activities in Vladimir.

There was a warm and cordial atmosphere at this second news conference. Clyde expressed his joy in returning to Vladimir and answered all the questions regarding the purpose and plans for this second Mission.

The response was overwhelming as the Drama Hall was packed for six services, each evening. Over 7,000 responded to the invitation to accept Christ. It was like the Book of Acts coming alive.

Six months earlier, when Dupin arrived in Vladimir there were only three, small evangelical churches. Two new churches were planted after the first Crusade. New churches are being planned and converts from the first Crusade were workers in planning the second mission. It was a great joy to see these new converts growing in Christ.

Dr. Wesley Phillips and Dr. Robert Schrocring visited hospitals, spoke to medical staffs and presented each hospital with thousands of dollars worth of antibiotics and other medicines provided by the Clyde Dupin Ministries.

Tom James, Overseas Crusade Director, was able to arrange for Dr. Dupin to do a one hour prime-time T.V. special which had 1.7 million viewers. The newspapers gave front page coverage. The evangelist was interviewed on a popular T.V. show and his mission made the news nightly.

They came to the Crusade by train, bus and many walked. Neither did they leave empty handed. Over 20,000 Bibles and booklets were distributed. One man about forty years old, took a Bible from a team member. He glanced at the cover and discovered it was a Bible. After being assured that it was God's Word he began crying, held it to his lips while he kissed the cover. He clutched it to his breast lovingly while admiring it with tender eyes.

"Thank you, thank you," he said. " This is the first time I have ever held a Bible in my hand!"

Tula

In April 1993, the Team experienced a successful Crusade in Tula, a Communist city 100 miles south of Moscow with a population of one million. Tula, the munitions capitol of the former Soviet Union was hit hardest by the Chernobyl nuclear accident a few years before, killing all the grass and leaves on the trees. The reception was very warm and each night at the Palace of Culture, hundreds came to hear the Gospel and receive Christ as personal Savior.

Among the Team members who accompanied Dr. Dupin on this Tula Crusade was Dean Andersen, stage manager for Oprha Winfrey. He was the camera man for this Crusade.

Second Crusade in Tula

The Team returned to Tula for a second Crusade in September 1993. Pastor Paul, of the Tula Seventh Day Adventist Church, and Mike Moror, the Russian Evangelistic Director for all Adventist work in Russia welcomed the Team warmly. It was through the prayers and encouragement of these two men that Dr. Dupin agreed to return to Tula.

Both of these godly men suffered much under the iron fist of Communism. Much of their ministry had to be in the underground house church. Pastor Paul was ridiculed, punished and made to go without food and forced to serve the Red Army, all because of his religious convictions.

But, the hard line Communists were back in control when Dupin returned. They were very unhappy with his presence. Orders had been given to officials at the Palace of Culture, where the meetings were to be conducted, not to open the doors for the well advertised Crusade. The evening newspaper had called the services illegal and told the people not to attend.

Just hours before the service was to begin a conference was arranged with Dupin and the mayor. Clyde began with a genuine respect for the mayor's beliefs, even though they were in direct contrast to his own. He also, listened with courtesy and understanding before he presented, in his persuasive way, why he had come back to Tula, not to change their political structure, but to bring the message of hope through Jesus Christ.

It wasn't long before the mayor began to relax, then smile and an awkward confrontation was defused. Their meeting ended on such a warm and friendly note the mayor agreed to host a press conference for Dr. Dupin the next day. Approval was finally given two hours before service time to let the doors open. The people came that night until the large auditorium overflowed

As usual, Dupin delivered a strong Gospel message. He explained how they could be forgiven and have peace with God. Suzanne Johnson, a former Miss Illinois and talent winner in Miss America Pageant, was soloist for the Tula crusade. She had worked with a Russian missionary living in Wheaton, Illinois, who taught her to sing in their mother tongue. The crowd was spellbound as they heard her sing.

While the Doors were Open

In addition to Vladimir and Tula, while the doors were open, Dr. Dupin conducted two major Crusades in the large textile city of Ivonna. His last two were held in Murom, one of the oldest and most beautiful cities in Russia

When the Dupin Team left Murom on May 1, 1996, there was a foreboding feeling that the doors for evangelism might not remain open much longer.

The Doors Close

Ignoring appeals from religious leaders around the world, Russian President Boris Yeltsin, signed a law in October, 1997, sharply curtailing religious activities and closing the door for Crusades.

"I'm sorry the doors have closed," Clyde said. "But I rejoice that over 37,500 people came to Christ and 100,000 Bibles were distributed through our ministry in Russia. Only heaven will tell the total results.

"I'm so thankful for the many friends that have invested their money over the years to make this ministry possible. I would have gone even more if the funds had been available", Clyde says.

God's Work Marches On

Clyde is a man of God. He is a minister of the Gospel to the whole world; an evangelist with a heart of love who rejoices in the salvation of the lost.

"My long-term goal in life has been a clear and direct one," Dupin states. "Since I was a young boy that goal has been to persuade the greatest possible number of people to commit their lives to Jesus Christ. That is my goal today as it was when He first called me to preach the Gospel. I pursue it with every ounce of energy I have. I always will. That is the reason I went to Russia, with great joy, to preach the Gospel where it had not been preached freely in over 70 years."

17

Bosnia - Mission of Hope

In the Bosnian village of Biljani the bus stopped. Dr. Dupin and the members of his team exited. There in the center of town the temporary green board markers had just been replaced with tall white marble stones, paid for by Iran. These white stones marked the grave sites of more than 350 Muslim men and children. All the men in Biljani had been brutally executed, by the Serbs, except one who escaped.

The small village school that once stood near this mass grave site, had been torn down, due to many horrendous acts of brutality, torture, rape and killings which had taken place there. The village women came out of their homes to talk of their grief.

Grace put her arms around one woman who stood with tears running down her cheeks. "We are all like orphans," the woman said. "Our husbands and children have been killed and our town is dead; all I can do is sit and cry. We have no future, no dreams."

Hope For Bosnia

Clyde said, "One of the main goals in my going to Bosnia was to proclaim the Gospel of Jesus Christ and give the people hope."

In this land where the Apostle Paul and other early church fathers, supposedly, planted the seeds of the Gospel, the doors which have long been closed are once again opening for evangelism. After centuries of strife, conflict and the recent civil war (1992-1996), Dupin felt this would be the right time to share the message of faith, hope and forgiveness through Jesus Christ. Why Bosnia?

Wes, Dr. Dupin's son, (pastor of Daybreak Community Church, Hudsonville, Michigan) visited the Balkins on a humanitarian mission with Joel Samy, president of World Hope in February, 1997. Upon Wes' return home, he called his father. "Dad, the people of Bosnia need your ministry! This land is without God! I think you should consider going to Bosnia and Croatia."

"Wes, since the doors seem to be closing in Russia", Clyde answered, "This may be where God wants us to do our next overseas mission. I will give prayerful consideration to your suggestion".

A few weeks later Clyde received a call from Joel Samy asking if he could come to Kernersville to discuss the possibility of Crusades in Bosnia, Herzegovina, and Croatia in 1998. Joel told Dupin he would soon be moving his family to Zagreb, Croatia, to spend the next year doing missionary work. Joel agreed to work with Tom James, Dupin's Overseas Crusade Director, in preparation for Crusade Celebrations in Bosnia and Croatia.

Mission of Hope

Weeks before Dupin was to leave for Bosnia and Croatia on the Mission of Hope, he had asked friends across America to join him in a day of fasting and prayer on April 15, 1998. He would need God's power and protection as never needed before for a Mission of this magnitude.

On April 17, 1998 before boarding the plane in Newark, New Jersey to fly to Zagreb, Croatia, Clyde gathered the group of 25 for prayer.

Arrangements had been made by the U.N. Special Forces to have a military escort to meet the Dupin team at the Zagreb airport to assist in getting them and the $60,000.00 in medical supplies, through customs. Soon they were all through customs along with the many large boxes of medicines, without a hitch.

Bosnia

Sunday dawned a beautiful sunny day. After an early morning worship service, Dupin and his team boarded their bus for Sanski Most, Bosnia. Waiting at the Croatian-Bosnian border was Major James Seawood, from the U.S. Army. He was their escort, provided by the U.N. Special Forces, for the entire Dupin Mission.

The Sana River separates Croatia from Bosnia at this border. The bridge over into Bosnia was a new one because all the bridges had been destroyed during the war. Not only had the bridges been demolished, but 200,000 people were killed, 250,000 were wounded and three million became homeless refugees.

Sanski Most

The Dupin bus rolled into Sanski Most about 5:00 p.m. Their group had now grown from 25 to 35. Ten more had joined the group in Zagreb to be a working part of the Team. These new members included Joel and Shelia Samy, four translators and Joel Hill, from Mission Network News, who reported daily on Dupin's activities on 950 radio stations throughout the world.

At 8:00 p.m. Clyde and Grace hosted a banquet for Mayor Alagic, his wife and several government leaders. The entire Dupin team was a part of this occasion, with saxophonist Donnie Haulk playing several songs during the meal.

Mayor Alagic was a warm and friendly individual. He and Clyde hit it off immediately, enjoying their meal and fellowship. During the course of the meal, the Muslim mayor leaned over and said, "Dr. Dupin, tomorrow I would like to take you and your wife to my home village. I want you to meet my mother."

The Dupins were happy to accept this special invitation. The next morning at 9:00 a.m., the mayor was at the hotel with a car and driver. His personal cameraman came to record the event.

The once beautiful country side that led to the Mayor's village, was now scarred by bombed homes and buildings.

The Mayor's elderly mother met the Dupins at the door of her newly rebuilt house. The old home had been destroyed during the war. This gentle Muslim woman wept as she told how she and her husband were abused by the Serbian soldiers.

"They came into my home", she said. "They stripped off my clothes and searched my body for gold. Not only that," she continued, "They took my husband out into the yard, made him get down on all fours and eat grass. They beat him so hard he died later." Tears coursed down her checks as she related this story to the Dupins.

These stories of terrible atrocities were heard by the Dupin Team everywhere they went in Bosnia.

First Service

By 7:00 p.m. the gymnasium was nearly full with over a 1,000 present. A Muslim priest from the local Mosque sat on the front row to keep watch on these events. He led a delegation of several students who were, apparently, trained to disrupt the meeting.

It was evident Dupin had studied the Muslim religion and had a good understanding of Bosnian culture. He had worked diligently on his sermon to make the Gospel as clear and simple as possible.

Clyde preached with much tact and wisdom. Knowing the pain, hurt and hopelessness these people had suffered, his first message was "Hope in a Hopeless World." He explained how we can know God through His son Jesus Christ.

When the invitation was given 45 young people came forward to accept Christ. Their peers hissed and called out "boos." Each person who came forward was counseled with personally and then given a Bible to keep as their own.

There were several older teenagers who were on the verge of going forward, but were restrained by the jeers of other Muslims who were in attendance.

The second night's service in Sanski Most was smaller. Certainly, it was evident the Muslim priest had organized a protest against Dupin and his message of salvation through Jesus Christ. The "boos" and "cat calls" were much louder this night. Still Clyde continued with his message of hope, without a moment's hesitation.

Clyde not only took a message of hope to the Bosnian people, but the Clyde Dupin Ministries provided $60,000.00 of medicine and medical supplies. Dr. Wesley Phillips and Dr. Everett Conrad (board members of Clyde Dupin Ministries), presented these many boxes of antibiotics and other pharmaceuticals to the Sanski Most Hospital.

Other team members went into the schools inviting the students to attend the evening "Celebration." Donnie Haulk would play a lively number on his sax and Suzanne would sing.

While Dr. Dupin was in Sanski Most a press conference was hosted by Mayor Alagica. "I have come from America with a message of hope," Clyde stated. "I know your people have been hurt deeply. But there is hope." This was the prayer Clyde had in his heart as he left Sanski Most, "God, give hope to these hopeless people."

Sarajevo

On Wednesday, the team boarded the bus for Sarajevo, the capitol city of Bosnia. It was once a very beautiful city nestled between surrounding mountains. The once proud city that had hosted the 1984 Winter Olympics, now lay in ruins. The entire downtown area was totally devastated.

Major Seawood pointed out a wall with the message "Welcome to hell." Truly it was a hellish place. The stadium was in ruins, land mines throughout the city were a constant danger. It was shocking to see the ravages of war.

Deputy Commander Colonel Michael Khure and Colonel Jackson, Chief of Chaplains, met the Dupin team in the newly rebuilt Holiday Inn. He, along with other military personnel, led the way up a mountainous street to a Catholic orphanage. This was a large four-story building that had been bombed eight times during the war. The nuns were trying to restore it. Mark Sweezie and Denny Jonker, from Daybreak Community Church, presented Sister Aberata $11,000.00 to help in the restoration of the orphanage.

Mostar

Snow capped mountains, beautiful lakes, lush green valleys made for a very beautiful drive to Mostar. This city is in the Southern part of Bosnia, known as Herzegovina, was hard hit in the war. It is still a very dangerous city controlled by the Mafia. Because of the present danger, the Ero Hotel, where the team stayed had a manned armored tank across the street and armed soldiers at each door.

In this city of 100,000 people, there are only two small evangelical churches. Karmelo Kresonja, Clyde's translator, pastors one of these churches.

Mostar Celebration

It was threatening rain when Dupin entered the bombed out theater where the evening Celebration Rally was held. The theater was totally blacked out except for a few 500 watt bulbs on the stage. There were no seats, no heat, just hard, rough cement. More than 700 people stood for the service.

Pastor Kresonja's church people had prayed all day for this special night.

Dr. Dupin brought a simple salvation message. When he gave the invitation 120 people, of all ages, responded by coming forward to accept Christ. It was a night to remember.

Zagreb, Croatia

After a very successful rally in Mostar, Dupin returned to Zagreb for Saturday and Sunday night Celebrations. On Saturday morning Tom James was very concerned because there was a rumor and a headline story in the leading Sarajevo newspaper which was very critical of Dupin for being allowed to preach in the all Muslim city of Sanski Most.

There were even some threats made on his life. It was suggested that maybe the last two Celebrations in Zagreb be canceled. After prayer and much discussion with Tom, Wes, Major Seawood, Joel and local officials, Clyde said, "I have come here to preach the Gospel and I am not afraid. The

Saturday night youth rally and Sunday night Celebration will go on as planned."

There were many young people in attendance for the Youth Rally in the outdoor sports arena. McDonald's restaurants gave sponsorship to this event by giving free orange juice and balloons and placed a Celebration invitation on every food tray. The Baptist pastor, a Catholic priest and the Serbian Orthodox priest were seated on the platform, at the rally, in support of Dr. Dupin.

Clyde's message for the youth was appropriately based on the story of the rich young ruler in the Bible, Mark 10. This young man asked the right question of Jesus, and received the right answer; but the young man made the wrong decision in not following Him. Clyde also shared contemporary stories about Princess Diana and the current movie "Titanic".

When the invitation was given there were about 40 youth who came forward to make decisions for Christ.

The Sunday evening "Celebration" was in the beautiful Grand Ballroom of the Sheraton Hotel. There was a large grand piano for Bob Andersen to play.

It was a thrill to see more than six hundred people who represented every stratum of society fill the room. They were touched by Clyde's message and many had tears streaming down their cheeks as they came forward. There was applause by the audience when the seekers responded to the invitation. It was a wonderful closing service to conclude the "Mission of Hope."

The Future

Evangelism has always been the very heartbeat of Dupin's ministry. It is what God has called him to do. The farm boy from near Elizabethtown, Kentucky, had a dream that has taken him to more than 40 countries. This dream has included over 400 Crusades and brought four million people to hear him preach the Gospel.

Clyde Dupin has also stayed on the cutting edge of world evangelism. He has always attempted great things for God and expected great things from God. He has been effective because of
his faith in God and a firm commitment to proclaim the inspired Word of God. The Bible has always been his textbook.

More than anything else, Clyde yearns for people around the world to know Jesus Christ as their personal Savior. In a changing world, he proclaims the timeless message which he believes is for every generation.

Even though his ministry spans almost half of this century, he looks forward, with excitement and enthusiasm, to sharing Christ in the 21st Century.

18

This I Believe

Author Bob Hill interviewed Dr. Clyde Dupin concerning some very important subjects. The following is the result of that 1998 interview.

QUESTION: *HOW DO YOU FEEL ABOUT THE SPIRITUAL CLIMATE IN AMERICA TODAY?*
ANSWER: I sense that there is a great spiritual vacuum in the lives of our people. In more than 40 years of full-time ministry I have never seen a greater hunger for the Gospel. I am seeing more people come to Christ in our ministry than ever before. In one year, I saw 20,000 in our crusades respond to the invitation to accept Christ.

At the same time, I see a great increase in evil of every kind. We have so many social problems such as our eleven million alcoholics. Since the Supreme Court ruling on abortion in 1973, millions of babies have been killed. Homosexuality is becoming more prevalent. Many of our TV programs feature violence and illicit sex. Evil seems to be more out in the open. I see the wheat and tares growing together. Only real spiritual awakening will save our nation.

QUESTION: *WHAT DO YOU BELIEVE IS OUR NUMBER ONE PROBLEM IN AMERICA?*

ANSWER: I believe our greatest problem is a breakdown in the family. There is no substitute for the home. God planned and ordained that there should be a family structure. Today we have about 60 million families. Each year there are more than one million divorces. This is frightening.

A recent study said that more than 51% of all marriages end in the divorce courts. It is tragic and heartbreaking when 1/3 of our children do not live with both parents. At the present time over half the births in Washington, D. C. are illegitimate.

QUESTION: *DO YOU BELIEVE THERE IS ANY WAY TO SAVE OUR HOMES?*

ANSWER: Yes. I believe Christ is the answer to the home problem. Families that pray together and attend church together are more likely to stay together. I have heard that when families pray and read the Bible together regularly there is only one divorce in 500 marriages. The national average is five divorces for every ten marriages. In all my crusades I preach on the importance of the Christian home.

As a pastor, I constantly preached and tried to teach my people the importance of a good Christian home. I don't think we are speaking out against divorce enough. It is wrong and hurts everyone involved. I think we need more teaching and preaching on family relationships. If we lose our homes, we lose everything good in this life. We must never forget God's divine ideal is one man for one woman until separated by death. Our TV programs and educational system have made a goddess of sex; but with all our permissiveness and adultery it hasn't brought happiness, peace, or joy to the human heart and mind.

I have seen many homes put back together through

the forgiveness and love of Christ. I sincerely believe that Christ is the answer to our broken homes.

QUESTION *WHAT IS YOUR HONEST OBSERVATIONS REGARDING OUR YOUTH TODAY?*
ANSWER: I meet a lot of wonderful, clean, wholesome, young people who love Christ. I also see a much larger group of youth who are searching. I often hear them say, "Nobody cares about me." "Life has no meaning or purpose." Many feel trapped and alienated from God, family, and sometimes their peer group. I think this is why many take drugs and try sex. I think people like Freddie Prinze and Elvis Presley, and John Belushi were examples of this kind of frustration and loneliness. I sometimes feel this generation of youth has been betrayed.

QUESTION: *WHAT DO YOU MEAN BY BEING BETRAYED?*
ANSWER: I probably should answer that in three parts. According to a recent study, 77% of college age young people said the church has no meaning for them. However, the majority believed in God. I think our young people want to hear preachers who really believe the Bible and preach with conviction and sincerity. I think they are interested in the supernatural and personal Christianity. Too often when they have gone to church they have heard a social gospel and Christ has not been lifted up.

Jesus said, "And I, if I be lifted up will draw all men unto me." Only Christ can forgive our sins and relieve our guilt. Too often the church has betrayed them.

Our youth have been betrayed by our educational system. I attended school back when the Bible was read and it was alright to pray. I believe when the Supreme Court prohibited voluntary prayer they violated the First Amendment's guarantee of the free exercise of religion. This encouraged the religion of secular humanism, which is very much a part of our educational system today. We took God out of our public schools and put violence, sex, drugs, and rebellion in His place. As long as we told our young people God was important and His Word was relevant, it seemed to have a wholesome effect on young people.

It seems we train the head and let the heart run wild. We allow culture and character to walk miles apart. We don't seem to see the difference between knowledge and wisdom. In Proverbs 9:10 it says, "The fear of the Lord is the beginning of wisdom; and the knowledge of the holy is understanding."

Thirdly, many parents have failed to love and spend time with their children. They have failed to discipline. A recent survey indicates that the average father spends 37 seconds a day in real conversation with his young son.

When 1/3 of our children do not live with both parents how can they be complete and happy? What chance does those who are born out of wedlock have for a good life? A juvenile judge said, "I have never had a wayward girl before me who was loved by her father."

I believe every child deserves a happy Christian home. Parents who sow to the wind in rearing their children will reap a whirlwind of regret and heartache.

QUESTION: *HOW DO YOU FEEL ABOUT YOUR OWN CHILDREN TODAY?*

ANSWER: I have often said if I won the world for Christ and lost my children I would be a failure. Grace and I always tried to show love and spend time with our children. I believe we were firm in our discipline and probably could be called strict parents. We always had Bible reading and prayer with them daily. As a family we always had a lot of fun together. I am proud of my three children, for they are all very committed Christians and each are married to Christian companions. Our oldest son, Wes, was associated with me in my ministry for 15 years and now pastors a large church in Hudsonville, Michigan. Ken pastors a church in Columbia, South Carolina, and often assists me in our crusades. Our daughter, Joy, and her husband, Scott George, are committed Christians and live in Greenville, South Carolina. We have eight grandchildren and two are preparing for full time ministry.

QUESTION: *HOW DO YOU FEEL ABOUT THE FUTURE OF YOUR MINISTRY?*

ANSWER: I have spent more than 40 years in full-time ministry, and unless Christ returns I believe I will have many more years. I think of myself as a God-called evangelist. Evangelism is my calling, it's my mission, it's my life. I would preach a lifetime for the joy of seeing one person come to Christ. I believe I was born to preach. I was called to preach early in life and never considered doing anything else.

QUESTION: *YOU HAVE PREACHED TO GREAT CROWDS AND HAVE SEEN THOUSANDS COME TO CHRIST. IS THERE SOME SECRET, OR HOW DO YOU EXPLAIN YOUR WORLDWIDE MINISTRY?*

ANSWER: I honestly can't explain it. There are many men more gifted and better qualified. The opportunities I have had such as preaching to 45,000 people almost frightens me. Perhaps I know my limitations and human weaknesses and this makes me depend absolutely on the Holy Spirit. Whatever success I have had is only a miracle of a loving God.

Early in my Christian life I made a total surrender to God. I am not perfect, but I feel I discovered the secret of a Spirit-filled life. This to me was death to the self-life and a total surrender to obey and do God's will. It was a crisis experience for me.

More than 40 years ago I committed myself to a daily, disciplined prayer life. I immediately discovered greater power in my preaching and especially in giving the invitation. I discovered through prayer there was nothing too hard for God to do. I began to expect miracles as a result of prayers and they began to happen. I purposed to give God the very best and all of whatever talents I might have. One hundred percent of my time and energy would be dedicated to God and His work. I have no sidelines or money-making involvements. The sharing of the Gospel is my life. I have never given myself to moonlighting or secular employment since college days.

QUESTION: *HOW DO YOU FEEL ABOUT THE BIBLE?* ANSWER: I have faith to believe the Bible is without error. I accept it as the inspired Word of God. It is my textbook. I believe in the deity of Christ, the Virgin Birth, the Atonement, the Resurrection and coming again of Jesus Christ. It is my authority for all I believe and preach.

QUESTION: *WHAT IS YOUR FAVORITE VERSE?* ANSWER: I have several. Each morning when I awake I like to condition my mind with briefly meditating on "This is the day which the Lord hath made; I will rejoice and be glad in it." (Psalm 118:24); and, "Thou will keep him in perfect peace, whose mind is stayed on thee: because he trusteth in thee." (Isaiah 26:3).

I often write Psalm 37:5 when I sign my name. It is a favorite verse: "Commit thy way unto the Lord, trust also in him; and he shall bring it to pass." When I face challenges, I draw strength and faith from Philippians 4:13, "I can do all things through Christ which strengtheneth me." If it's a big decision, I turn to Proverbs 3:5-6, "Trust in the Lord with all thine heart; and lean not unto thine own understanding. In all thy ways acknowledge Him and He shall direct thy paths."

When in prayer I like Jeremiah 33:3, "Call unto me, and I will answer thee, and show thee great and mighty things, which thou knowest not." I love the Bible, I read the Bible and I believe it. For years I have tried to read one new book a week and regularly subscribe to about 35 religious and news magazines. But there is no substitute for the Bible. I find I am better and my preaching is more effective as I spend more time in the Word.

QUESTION: *WHAT ARE THE MAJOR INVOLVEMENTS OF YOUR PERSONAL MINISTRY?*
ANSWER: I think of my major ministry as the city-wide interdenominational crusades. I have two full-time crusade directors, who are constantly preparing for these crusades. I do about eight major crusades each year. In these crusades, Rick Webb directs the music program.

My wife, Grace, conducts Ladies Teas each morning in all our crusades. This has been a tremendous ministry to the ladies. She has had over 1,000 ladies at a single Tea. I speak each year at many prayer breakfasts, banquets, evangelism conferences and various conventions and on college campuses.

The office operation and large amounts of mail takes considerable time. For many years I have written a newspaper column, "Religious Viewpoint," which appears in about 85 newspapers throughout America. It's a busy life, but I enjoy it and have a wonderful family and team to assist me.

I am not an independent evangelist. Our-crusades are Christ-centered and church-centered to conserve results. I don't know why, but I have often been called "the evangelist with a pastor's heart." My evangelistic preaching is a simple salvation message. I preach for a verdict. I preach that Christ is the answer. I believe our world is too dangerous for anything but truth, too small for anything but love. I talk about God's love, forgiveness and a new life. I preach the cross and that everyone can be born again. I feel an urgency to get this message to the most possible people in the shortest possible time. I believe crusade evangelism is one of the best ways to reach the masses.

QUESTION: *YOU HAVE COMMITTED YOUR WHOLE LIFE TO EVANGELISM. HAVE YOU EVER DOUBTED THAT DECISION?*
ANSWER: No, I've enjoyed every day of it. I have known since my teenage preaching years that I am essentially an evangelist. I pastored for ten years, but I have always been an evangelistic preacher. By talent, though small, and by burden and by choice I am an evangelist. Even during my years as a pastor I saw over 2,000 people respond to the invitation in my church. I have always wanted to be a soul winner above everything else.

I have had opportunities to do many kinds of ministries, but evangelism is my first love. I like to see churches work together in interdenominational evangelism. This type of evangelism brings renewal to the church and reaches many with the Good News, who will never attend a local church. I encourage pastors to let their denominational fences be low enough to reach out and join hearts and hands with other churches in evangelism. I encourage them to magnify their agreements and minimize their differences for the sake of lost souls.

QUESTION: *ONE FINAL QUESTION. AS WE ENTER THE 21ST CENTURY, HOW DO YOU VIEW THE WORLD SITUATION?*

ANSWER: In my travels throughout the world, I sense the veneer of civilization is very thin. There is a real battle between the forces of good and evil. There is a global insecurity, faltering economies, a new wave of terrorism, and a great spiritual hunger. People everywhere seem frightened as they face the future.

I believe Christ is the only hope to save us from destruction. I believe each new generation needs to hear the saving message of Jesus Christ. There are 5.8 billion people on planet earth. Even in this information age, 3 billion are still unreached for Christ.

I think the Christian world is in a spiritual crisis. There is a wave of compromise in many evangelical churches where self-esteem, pop-psychology, and worldly entertainment have become a substitute for the Gospel. The Gospel message is non-negotiable. Our culture must never become more powerful than our Gospel. America needs a spiritual renewal which could change our nation and touch the world for Christ.

It is my strong belief that Christ will soon return. What we do to reach our lost world, we must do now. Our permissive society has invaded the lives of many Christians and created apathy and lukewarmness toward world evangelism. My MISSION will alway be to fulfill the Great Commission. "Go ye into all the world, and preach the gospel to every creature." (Mark 16:15)

For further information write to:
Clyde Dupin Ministries
P.O. Box 565
Kernersville, N.C. 27285